Information Systems in Child, Youth, and Family Agencies: Planning, Implementation, and Service Enhancement

Information Systems in Child, Youth, and Family Agencies: Planning, Implementation, and Service Enhancement

Anthony J. Grasso
Irwin Epstein
Editors

The Haworth Press, Inc.
New York · London · Norwood (Australia)

Information Systems in Child, Youth, and Family Agencies: Planning, Implementation, and Service Enhancement has also been published as *Child & Youth Services,* Volume 16, Number 1 1993.

The Haworth Press, Inc., 10 Alice Street, Binghamton, NY 13904-1580 USA

Library of Congress Cataloging-in-Publication Data

Information systems in child, youth, and family agencies: planning, implementation, and service enhancement / Anthony J. Grasso, Irwin Epstein, editors.
     p. cm.
   Issued also as Vol. 16, No. 1 of Child & youth services.
   Includes bibliographical references and index.
   ISBN 1-56024-465-8.–ISBN 1-56024-466-6 (pbk.)
     1. Youth–Services for–Michigan–Data processing–Case studies. 2. Boysville of Michigan.
I. Grasso, Anthony J. II. Epstein, Irwin.
HV1435.M5I54 1993
362.7′4′09774–dc20   93-16913
                                                          CIP

INDEXING & ABSTRACTING

Contributions to this publication are selectively indexed or abstracted in print, electronic, online, or CD-ROM version(s) of the reference tools and information services listed below. This list is current as of the copyright date of this publication. See the end of this section for additional notes.

- *Bulletin Signaletique*, INIST/CNRS-Service Gestion des Documents Primaires, 2, allee du Parc de Brabois, F-54514 Vandoeuvre-les-Nancy, Cedex, France

- *Cambridge Scientific Abstracts*, *Risk Abstracts,* Cambridge Information Group, 7200 Wisconsin Ave #601, Bethesda, MD 20814

- *Child Development Abstracts & Bibliography*, University of Kansas, 2 Bailey Hall, Lawrence, KS 66045

- *Criminal Justice Abstracts*, Willow Tree Press, 15 Washington Street, 4th Floor, Newark, NJ 07102

- *Criminology, Penology and Police Science Abstracts*, Kugler Publications bv, P. O. Box 11188, 1001 GD Amsterdam, The Netherlands

- *ERIC Clearinghouse on Elementary & Early Childhood Education*, University of Illinois, 805 West Pennsylvania Avenue, Urbana, IL 61801

- *Exceptional Child Education Resources (ECER), (online through DIALOG and hard copy)*, The Council for Exceptional Children, 1920 Association Drive, Reston, VA 22091

- *Index to Periodical Articles Related to Law*, University of Texas, 727 East 26th Street, Austin, TX 78705

(continued)

- *International Bulletin of Bibliography on Education*, Proyecto B.I.B.E./Apartado 52, San Lorenzo del Escorial, Madrid, Spain

- *Inventory of Marriage and Family Literature (online and hard copy)*, National Council on Family Relations, 3989 Central Avenue NE, Suite 550, Minneapolis, MN 55421

- *Mental Health Abstracts (online through DIALOG)*, IFI/Plenum Data Company, 3202 Kirkwood Highway, Wilmington, DE 19808

- *OT BibSys*, American Occupational Therapy Foundation, P. O. Box 1725, Rockville, MD 20849-1725

- *Psychological Abstracts (PsycINFO)*, American Psychological Association, P. O. Box 91600, Washington, DC 20090-1600

- *Referativnyi Zhurnal (Abstracts Journal of the Institute of Scientific Information of the Republic of Russia)*, The Institute of Scientific Information, Baltijskaja ul., 14, Moscow A-219, Republic of Russia

- *Sage Family Studies Abstracts*, Sage Publications, Inc., 2455 Teller Road, Newbury Park, CA 91320

- *Social Planning/Policy & Development Abstracts (SOPODA)*, Sociological Abstracts, Inc., P. O. Box 22206, San Diego, CA 92192-0206

- *Social Work Research & Abstracts*, National Association of Social Workers, 750 First Street NW, 8th Floor, Washington, DC 20002

- *Sociological Abstracts (SA)*, Sociological Abstracts, Inc., P. O. Box 22206, San Diego, CA 92192-0206

- *Sociology of Education Abstracts*, Carfax Publishing Company, P. O. Box 25, Abingdon, Oxfordshire OX14 3UE, United Kingdom

- *Studies on Women Abstracts*, Carfax Publishing Company, P. O. Box 25, Abingdon, Oxfordshire OX14 3UE, United Kingdom

(continued)

SPECIAL BIBLIOGRAPHIC NOTES

related to indexing and abstracting

☐ indexing/abstracting services in this list will also cover material in the "separate" that is co-published simultaneously with Haworth's special thematic journal issue or DocuSerial. Indexing/abstracting usually covers material at the article/chapter level.

☐ monographic co-editions are intended for either non-subscribers or libraries which intend to purchase a second copy for their circulating collections.

☐ monographic co-editions are reported to all jobbers/wholesalers/approval plans. The source journal is listed as the "series" to assist the prevention of duplicate purchasing in the same manner utilized for books-in-series.

☐ to facilitate user/access services all indexing/abstracting services are encouraged to utilize the co-indexing entry note indicated at the bottom of the first page of each article/chapter/contribution.

☐ this is intended to assist a library user of any reference tool (whether print, electronic, online, or CD-ROM) to locate the monographic version if the library has purchased this version but not a subscription to the source journal.

☐ individual articles/chapters in any Haworth publication are also available through the Haworth Document Delivery Services (HDDS).

Information Systems in Child, Youth, and Family Agencies: Planning, Implementation, and Service Enhancement

CONTENTS

SECTION TWO

SECTION THREE

ABOUT THE EDITORS

Anthony J. Grasso, DSW, is Director, School of Social Work, University of Nevada at Las Vegas School of Social Work. He was formerly Director of Boysville Institute. The author of several articles on research and information utilization in social work, he is the designer of the Boysville Management Information System and several other agency-based research and information systems.

Irwin Epstein, PhD, is Professor of Social Work Research at Hunter College School of Social Work. A former Fulbright Scholar at the University of Wales, he has taught social work research methods and their clinical and program applications at Howard University, the University of Michigan, and the University of Warwick, in addition to Hunter College. From 1987 to 1988, he served as the first occupant of the Institute Chair at Boysville of Michigan, for which he received the Hugh Whiffle Award from the Michigan Association of Childcare Agencies. He is the author of several books and articles on research and information utilization in social work.

Together Drs. Grasso and Epstein planned and co-convened the Conference on Research Utilization and have written several articles on agency-based research utilization. They have co-conducted computerization and program evaluation workshops in the United States and Canada. In addition, they serve as research utilization, management information, and evaluation consultants to several social agencies across the country.

Preface

Boysville of Michigan is a not-for-profit, multiservice agency for troubled adolescents and their families. It offers programs in residential care, community-based group homes, foster care, in-home care, and supervised independent living to youth who are placed in our care. Most are sent to us by the juvenile courts. The largest, private, youth-serving agency in Michigan, our clients come from all parts of the state to one of thirteen separate program locations. In addition to serving Michigan's youth, a Boysville site in Toledo provides services to children and families from nineteen counties in Ohio.

The articles that follow describe Boysville's five-year effort to design, implement and evaluate an agency-based, computerized management information, program evaluation, and clinical decision making system, BOMIS (Boysville Management Information System). Boysville's present treatment program is built upon the integration of four key interventive components: residential care, group work (while in residence), family work (while in residence through six months post-release), and education.

Broadly speaking, the goal of BOMIS is to promote the integration of these intervention programs through the collection, analysis, interpretation, and feedback of information relevant to practitioners' decision making needs at all levels and in all parts of the agency. This implies a range of possible uses of information from clinical decision making with a single youngster to supervisory decisions about workers, from evaluative decisions about total programs and accountability information for funding and accrediting bodies to external policy advocacy.

Why would a service agency embark on such an ambitious project?

[Haworth co-indexing entry note]: "Preface." Boylan, Brother Francis. Co-published simultaneously in *Child & Youth Services,* (The Haworth Press, Inc.) Vol. 16, No. 1, 1993, pp. xvii-xix; and: *Information Systems in Child, Youth, and Family Agencies: Planning, Implementation, and Service Enhancement* (ed: Anthony J. Grasso, and Irwin Epstein) The Haworth Press, Inc., 1993, pp. xiii-xv. Multiple copies of this article/chapter may be purchased from The Haworth Document Delivery Center. Call 1-800-3-HAWORTH (1-800-342-9678) between 9:00 - 5:00 (EST) and ask for DOCUMENT DELIVERY CENTER.

xiii

Several years ago, we recognized that accountability was becoming a central issue for human service agencies. Rather than viewing it as solely an external, bureaucratic requirement, however, our conception of accountability extended beyond the need to supply information to funders. Instead, it incorporated notions of responsibility to our workers, our profession, our supporting public, and above all, to our clients.

Thus, in our view, every human service organization must at least try to answer two profound, but deceptively simple questions. Are we really doing what we claim we are doing? And, if we are, does it work? The self-knowledge arrived at by attempting to answer these questions provides the informational base for our multidimensional view of accountability. BOMIS is a means for achieving this self-knowledge.

In contrast with other, more conventional accountability and/or management information systems, BOMIS is *line worker driven.* Thus, while others such as program managers and external funders benefit from the utilization of BOMIS information, its primary purpose is to serve the decision making needs of those who directly deliver services to Boysville youth and their families. Consequently, BOMIS technology and Boysville staff who are charged with its implementation are dedicated to providing timely, valid, reliable, and relevant information for ongoing treatment as it occurs.

Not surprisingly, the effort to make effective use of BOMIS also requires a unique and extensive commitment of internal agency resources to staff training and supervision. Our direct experience with BOMIS and our evaluative research on BOMIS strongly suggest that we cannot rely on professional education alone to prepare workers for its use. Consequently, BOMIS designers have had to devote considerable attention to the training of trainers and of supervisors. For these efforts to be effective, BOMIS also must provide information in a timely manner for training and supervisory use.

Clearly, such a complex system places heavy demands on its managers and implementors. These individuals must commit themselves to a disciplined use of information to guide decision making. At the same time, managers must allow workers to find their own solutions to problems which arise at every organizational level.

Thus, despite its use of information technology and its clinical emphasis, BOMIS does not provide diagnostic formulas or treatment prescriptions. It is not a substitute for qualitative clinical information, or for practice wisdom. Nor does it benefit from prescriptive management. Instead, it provides an informational context within which creative diagnostic, treatment, and management decisions can flourish. To achieve this, enough room must be given for workers to make mistakes, learn from these mistakes, and find new solutions through creative individual, collaborative, and team efforts. Advanced technology does not eliminate the need for the *artistic* aspect of practice. Ideally, it enhances it.

In some respects, the administrator of an information system is like a symphony conductor–important, but not terribly impressive without a well-integrated and functioning orchestra. The administrator's or conductor's task is to coordinate the various individual and group efforts, to draw out the best from everyone, to ensure harmony and build cooperation in the collective effort. The conductor's goal, of course, is to provide the most rewarding musical experience possible for the audience. Likewise the ultimate goal of the BOMIS effort is to provide the most beneficial experience for our clients, the youth in placement at Boysville and their families.

Having taken on this ambitious project, Boysville is now beginning to fully disseminate our experience with it. This collection of papers represents one aspect of our dissemination effort. This is not to imply, however, that the development of BOMIS has been completed. Actually, it is still at the very beginning stage of implementation and utilization. New informational components are currently being designed. New utilization problems and possibilities are constantly being raised in treatment, supervision, team collaboration, training, program design, program evaluation, information technology, and agency policy.

With these new challenges in mind, Boysville of Michigan and its dedicated staff remain committed to the multifaceted use of "state of the art" information technology for support of the highest quality, professional practice to achieve the best possible clinical and programmatic outcomes.

Brother Francis Boylan, csc
Executive Director
Boysville of Michigan

Introduction:
The Need for a New Model
of Information Utilization
in Human Service Agencies

Anthony J. Grasso
Irwin Epstein

ABSTRACT. In the past decade, human service agencies and the information systems they employ have become increasingly complex, as have the problems of the clients they serve. Administrative models indigenous to the social services, and social work education for new administrative roles, have not kept pace with these changes. As a result, many agencies have sought administrators trained outside the human services, with negative consequences. This paper calls for the development of new models of information utilization which are designed specifically for social service settings. This collection of papers describes Boysville of Michigan's effort to create such a model and demonstrates its utility.

Anthony J. Grasso is Director, School of Social Work, University of Nevada at Las Vegas, 4505 Maryland Parkway, Las Vegas, NV 89154-5032. Irwin Epstein is affiliated with the School of Social Work, Hunter College, City University of New York, 129 East 79th Street, New York, NY 10021. A portion of this paper was previously published in *Research Utilization in the Social Services: Innovations for Practice and Administration.* The Haworth Press, Inc.

[Haworth co-indexing entry note]: "Introduction: The Need for a New Model of Information Utilization in Human Service Agencies." Grasso, Anthony J., and Irwin Epstein. Co-published simultaneously in *Child & Youth Services,* (The Haworth Press, Inc.) Vol. 16, No. 1, 1993, pp. 1-13; and: *Information Systems in Child, Youth, and Family Agencies: Planning, Implementation, and Service Enhancement* (ed: Anthony J. Grasso, and Irwin Epstein) The Haworth Press, Inc., 1993, pp. 1-13. Multiple copies of this article/chapter may be purchased from The Haworth Document Delivery Center. Call 1-800-3-HAWORTH (1-800-342-9678) between 9:00 - 5:00 (EST) and ask for DOCUMENT DELIVERY CENTER.

1

Multiple problems confront today's human service agencies. These range from securing adequate funding to meeting the needs of increasingly difficult-to-serve clients. This multiplicity of problems has had varying impacts on agency functioning, one being that as client and organizational problems have become more complex and the technologies for dealing with them more specialized and differentiated, the practice of social work in agency settings has become more fragmented (Fabricant, 1985; Gruber, 1974). The effect has been poor service to clients and, as competing interests in agencies have vied for dominance and control, unresolved organizational conflicts.

At the same time, it is not uncommon to hear direct service practitioners complain that administrators at their agencies are more concerned with budget items than with the well-being of clients, or to hear agency administrators accuse line workers of failing to achieve on objective measures of program success. Add to these problems the additional strains put on agency operations by the introduction of a new information technology and it is no wonder that human service agencies are struggling to survive (Caputo, 1988).

Not only are agencies in difficulty, but so are social service administrators who, confronted with the daily pressures of these complex problems, find themselves ill-prepared to respond. Traditionally, the most common route to a career in social agency administration involved training in interpersonal practice, two or three years of post-Master's experience in an agency, promotion to a supervisory position and, after some years, to program management, and finally movement into agency administration (Patti & Austin, 1977). Thus, many of today's administrators in social agencies came to their positions with little or no formal training in administration. In the process of career development these administrators were socialized in social work values and trained in direct practice as well as supervisory skills.

This route to social agency administration was still organizationally syntonic when accountability requirements were simpler and funding sources more plentiful, and when human service organizations had single-service missions and technologies. But as social service systems, treatment, and information technologies became more complex and the competition for limited resources intensified, social work administrators were caught unprepared to deal with these changing conditions.

Since the field had not developed its own indigenous models of administrative practice, many social service organizations responded to this crisis by hiring individuals trained in administration in other fields. In so doing, these organizations have gained some prestige and administrative and/or technical expertise but, to a certain degree, they have subordinated a client service orientation to a concern for efficiency (Patti, 1985).

Clearly, administration as a practice specialty in social work has reached a critical stage over the past decade. A serious challenge confronts social work administration as to whether it represents a unique field of practice, separate from other forms of organizational administration (Patti, 1983). In this climate of confusion, more and more social work agencies are being headed by individuals with degrees in public administration, management studies, business administration, educational administration, public health administration, and human relations, to name the most prominent. If it is to remain a viable field of study, social work administration must differentiate itself in relation to other types of administration. Writing on this topic, Patti (1983) comments:

> ... the issue that confronts social work is whether it will take responsibility for defining the parameter of professional administrative practice in social welfare. ... The failure to do this in the years ahead will render social work a supplicant to the field of administration and blur the distinctive contribution its practitioners can make to furthering the effectiveness of social welfare organizations. (p. 19)

From an historical perspective, some of the root causes of the problems confronting the modern service agency can be identified. For example, the conflict identified above involving direct service practitioners and administrators finds its origins in the politics of scarcity in the 1970s that led to the application of management by objectives (MBO), public planning budgeting systems (PPBS), and cost-benefit analysis to human services with little or no regard for the effects on clients (Patti, 1983). This technological fragmentation of social services and social administration was not always the case. So, for example, discussing administrative practice in the 30s, Dunham (1939) notes that at that time, administrative practice was not ordinarily distinguished from direct practice nor thought of as a separate function. At that time, one could argue, it didn't need to be.

The introduction of complex accountability systems, information technology, and computerization has recently magnified the problem of service and administrative fragmentation. By focusing the agency on measurable aspects of program functioning and on routine reporting of these measures we have given greater emphasis to those forms of practice and to practice effects that are most amenable to quantitative measurement, thereby narrowing both agency focus and administrative conceptions of performance. Discussing the misuse of information technology, Clark (1985) remarks:

> Management information systems can be improved technically, but they are askew because their relationship to the organization is misunderstood. They are serving administrative decision making . . . [MIS systems] gather the wrong information, from the wrong sources, for the wrong users, at the wrong organizational level. (p. 71)

This misuse of information technology has resulted in new conflicts between direct service practitioners, supervisors, program managers, executives and information specialists such as computer programmers, program evaluators and systems managers.

It should be pointed out, however, that the separation of information gathering, analysis, and interpretation from those who apply it has not always characterized agency-based social work. Thus, for example, Tratner (1979) describes the way in which Jane Addams incorporated information collection, analysis and evaluation into her approach to direct practice.

No one would argue that separation of function and specialization isn't a valid response to current agency problems. Nor would anyone deny that dramatic changes have taken place from the times when agencies could best be characterized as loosely organized groups of volunteers working to address the "evils" of social injustice. Since then, however, the burgeoning social problems of the 1980s have forced social agencies to deal with increasingly complex and diverse internal and external environments. These conditions call for innovative solutions.

Not taking exception to the value of greater specialization and technological advance, this collection of articles is based on the assumption that when these technological processes are not integrated with a client service orientation, the resulting fragmentation has a negative effect on the agency, the direct service practitioner, and the client. On the other hand, when these powerful technological processes are effectively linked to agency structure and function, they offer the promise of much more effective and efficient service delivery.

Although an incremental strategy may be necessary to resolve issues too large to be resolved by single practice paradigms, the lack of a unifying vision leading to the integration of multiple frameworks of practice has been very costly to social work. In addition, the commonly held assumption that the resolution of single organizational problems somehow leads to the cumulative effect of resolving complex systemic problems has not helped.

Discussing paradigm shifts in other fields, Lincoln (1985) identifies a need for a new kind of organizational theory. She states:

> We have behaved as if the world was simply additive; that is, complex elements were simply aggregations of much simpler entities. We are now beginning to understand that systems are not merely the sum of more simple units; . . . (p. 34)

Similarly, in social work, there is a clear and urgent need to design and test practice models that successfully integrate advances in research, information technology, client treatment and service, supervision, training, and administration. Viewing this problem from a management perspective, several authors note the need for unifying themes to guide overall agency operations. Patti (1985), for example, sees the problem as resulting from lack of a clear, fundamental statement of purpose for social welfare administration and argues that service effectiveness should be the unifying philosophy of human service organizations. Rapp and Poertner (1987) agree and call for a shift in perspective that moves the client to "center stage" by focusing the assessment of agency performance on client outcome. Correlatively, Grasso and Epstein (1987) suggest that the value of helping clients should run across all levels of an organization and argue that by centering on improving staff skills at each level one can improve overall service effectiveness.

Each of the foregoing authors offers suggested strategies for mediating organizational conflicts and improving services in social work agencies. Patti sets a necessary tone for unifying organizational culture around the theme of service effectiveness, Rapp and Poertner use this to focus agency administration on the task of conceptualizing client-oriented agency performance, and Grasso and Epstein begin to address the issue of how to link staff skills development to the measurement of organizational performance.

Centering on the schism between information technology and social work practice, others have proposed strategies ranging from reconceptualizing the practitioner as an information specialist (Briar, 1980) to viewing the organization as a "host" site for a social work formulation of the research and development (R & D) function (Rothman, 1974). Those in social work who are influenced by decision theorists may search vainly for a mathematical formula, made conceivable by the advent of the computer, that, if found, would ensure totally rational decision making, would miraculously eliminate organizational conflicts, and would guide all practice decisions (Dickson, 1983).

Although computer technology moves us into directions of practice decision making and service restructuring unthought of a decade ago, it offers no magical solution to the problem of the fragmentation of social work practice. Nonetheless, it is still too early to negatively assess the impact of computers on social work practice.

In the 1960s and 1970s, computers in human service agencies were used primarily for accounting and record keeping. In the past 10 years, however, the impact has been much more extensive in that the computer is now seen as a tool to facilitate direct service with clients (Grasso & Epstein, 1987). Changes in the next 10 years should prove even more profound with the exploration of artificial intelligence and its application to social work practice (Henderson, 1986).

We cannot say whether or not these futuristic models of information processing will offer truly effective and viable solutions to the problems of fragmentation of practice. However, at this point in the evolving relationship of human service agency administration, clinical practice, and information technology, too many have come to the conclusion that computerization only adds to ours and our clients' problems.

The purpose of this book is to demonstrate that this negative judgement about the place of computers and information systems in social work agencies is, at the very least, premature, if not completely wrong.

More optimistically, it is our contention that it is possible to conceptually and organizationally integrate information technology, social service delivery, clinical practice, training, research, program evaluation, administration, policy and social work values into a single practice paradigm for social work. We view this as the central task of social work administration in the 1990s. Such an ideal integrative model, guided by basic social work values, would incorporate the most advanced information and treatment technologies available, but would center on the line level practitioner working with the client.

With regard to the implications for management information systems design, such an integration would rest on the following principles: (1) Administrative priority should be given to actual as well as measured performance. (2) Performance assessment should be based on valid and reliable information regarding *actual* performance of line staff. (3) In return for this information, line staff should receive information-feedback about clients that is timely and readily applicable to their practice. More generally, effective integration rests on the principle that one can only improve organizational performance by improving individual staff skill in effectively applying information at each level of the organization. This organizational principle is rooted in the assumption that the primary function of a social service agency is found in the exchange of information between the practitioner and the client, and that all other agency structures and processes must be designed to facilitate this exchange. If this assumption is correct, when conflicts in organizations exist they must be resolved around the informational and decision making requirements of the direct service worker and the client.

This special issue describes Boysville of Michigan's unique effort to integrate information technology and social work practice at every organizational level. In telling the story of this agency's innovative and far-reaching project, a number of problems emerge which are likely to face information specialists and social work administrators in other agencies that try to integrate information technology with the practice needs of direct service workers, and ultimately with the needs of clients. Overall, the goal of this collection of papers is to describe one agency-based attempt to integrate these technologies, structures and processes. While still unsure as to the complete list of elements required for successful integration, it is clear that how future human service organizations link performance, information processing, and conflict management will determine their capacity to perform effectively and efficiently.

BOYSVILLE OF MICHIGAN

Boysville of Michigan is the state's largest private agency serving troubled adolescents. Since its founding in 1948 with 15 boys, the agency has grown to now serve 550 boys and girls with treatment centers located at its main campus in Clinton, a smaller campus in Saginaw, and group homes in Detroit, Ecorse, Mt. Clemens, Redford, Saginaw, Mt. Morris, Alpena, and Monroe, Michigan, and in Toledo, Ohio.

Historically, Boysville's treatment technology was based on a modified version of positive peer culture in which the natural influences of the adolescent peer group were enlisted to bring about change in client behavior and attitude. Over the last few years, however, Boysville has expanded its intervention repertoire to include an intensive family therapy program on the main campus for all youth in placement, specialized foster care for youth unable to return to their natural family, and a metro area emergency placement program.

While a growing number of Boysville youth are neglected-abused, most are adjudicated delinquents with serious behavioral, social and educational problems. Most come from the tri-county Detroit area. Recently, in response to needs expressed by both the public and private sectors, Boysville expanded its mission to include services to girls.

BOYSVILLE'S NEED FOR AN INTEGRATED MANAGEMENT, INFORMATION, PRACTICE DECISION MAKING, PROGRAM EVALUATION AND APPLIED RESEARCH SYSTEM (BOMIS)

As with many social work organizations, Boysville began as a small agency adopting a "human relations" administrative approach (Etzioni, 1964) and a participatory management style. However, as the organization grew in size, structural complexity, and intervention repertoire, its non-hierarchical human relations ethos became increasingly problematic.

Although the mission and goals of Boysville were clearly articulated, prior to the implementation of BOMIS, efforts to fulfill this mission were often undermined by different professional staff working on different aspects of the program without a clear understanding of what their overall goals and objectives were. This led to specialties within the organization, such as education, treatment, dorm living, family services, etc., working towards conflicting individual client objectives, thereby subverting efforts at achievement of desired overall goals (Katz & Kahn, 1978).

This problem was intensified by lack of a clear specification of desired client outcome in the organization. Thus, different treatment specialties frequently tended to work toward achievement of client goals and objectives specific to their own expertise without any effort at treatment or programmatic integration (Perrow, 1974; Etzioni, 1960).

Because of conflicting definitions of goals and objectives, operations directors were faced daily with the necessity of making immediate and reactive decisions which often had a negative impact on the overall effectiveness of the organization. They did so without comprehending the organizational significance of these decisions.

Nevertheless, the human relations model comfortably fit with the religious orientation of the Holy Cross Brothers, employed by the Michigan Diocese to administer the agency. This fit manifested itself in administrative staff's genuine concern for the well-being of "co-workers" and in the continuing effort to promote the idea of a "work community" at Boysville. Human relations motivational theory functioned as an ideological underpinning to all organizational decision making.

However, the human relations ideology and its associated management style caused a great deal of uncertainty and ambiguity with regard to decision making at Boysville. It offered no clear delineation of roles or responsibilities at different levels of the organization. As a result, most conflicts in the organization were viewed as personality conflicts rather than structural problems that might be resolved by a rational, analytic, organizational process (Katz & Kahn, 1966).

As the organization grew, it became more decentralized, with sub-units of varying size located throughout the state. A conflict inevitably emerged between a need for uniformity across programs and a need for responsiveness to local differences. Those at the executive level of the organization concerned with finances, control, and personnel issues, tended to favor standardization and centralization (Handy, 1976). Resistance to this pressure came from the regional directors who favored decentralization and organizational diversity. Despite pressures toward centralization from some individuals on the executive staff, the prevailing ideological commitment to a human relations model prevailed for some time.

Nonetheless, as Boysville became more technologically complex, staff size increased as well as professional skill and diversity. With this increase in skill, specialization, and diversity came demands for higher quality and more specialized information that would facilitate practice decision making of various kinds at different levels in the organization by different kinds of practitioners.

These specialized needs for practice-based information coincided with an increased need of central administration for quantitative program information for internal administrative decision making as well as for external accountability and program expansion. As Katz and Kahn predicted (1966), the greater the distance between the higher and the lower levels in an organization, the greater the dependence upon quantitative versus qualitative information in decision making. This greater dependency on quantitative information for decision making was also consistent with the need felt by some at the executive level for greater uniformity and standardization within the organization.

Because of changes mentioned above, the treatment system at Boysville gradually became fragmented, uncoordinated and unintegrated with specialties independently pursuing their own institutional priorities and goals. This meant, for example, that family workers tended to be exclusively interested in family process and saw their specialty as the central intervention approach of the agency. The same was true of group workers, childcare workers, teachers, and so on. In addition, the work at different Boysville sites varied markedly because of the unique history and staffing patterns at these sites.

Officially, the coordinating body for each treatment unit was the treatment team. A treatment team was made up of one core teacher, two treatment specialists, a group leader and one family worker for every twelve children in care. The teams met weekly and reviewed treatment plans and process as well as developed an interdisciplinary treatment plan for each client that was to be monitored and updated on an ongoing basis while the child was in care. The treatment director (group therapist) in the program had traditionally been given informal authority to coordinate the efforts of the different treatment specialties on the team, but formally, they were seen as co-equal with all other team members. This structural contradiction, explained by the prevailing human relations orientation of the agency, subverted the coordination function of the treatment directors. In other words, they were given the responsibility for coordinating treatment at the team level, but they did not possess the formal authority to implement treatment decisions across different treatment specialties.

Higher level decision making was equally fragmented and contradictory. Despite the participatory ideology, the Executive Office generally made major agency decisions unilaterally. This might have been appropriate in a small, undifferentiated, centralized setting. At Boysville, however, it meant uncoordinated decision making throughout the agency. Thus, in 1982 Boysville had no long-range strategic plan in place, and most decisions were made on an *ad hoc* basis. And, because of an informal structure which allowed lower-level managers easy access to the Executive Office, there was a great deal of pressure for immediate responses to problems as opposed to planful, coordinated problem resolution.

This is not unique to Boysville, Katz and Kahn (1966), for example, remark:

> Immediate pressure often seems so overriding to executives that they will accept some hasty solutions and bypass a thorough analysis of the problem and the careful weighing of the likely major consequences of their action. The objective circumstances may be of such an emergency nature, that decisive actions must be embarked upon immediately. Often, however, specific organizational pressure and personality considerations are responsible for a decision being reached without an adequate analysis of the problem, or an intelligent assessment of the consequences. (p. 275)

From its external environment, Boysville was at this time experiencing pressure to change as well. In 1983, the Michigan Department of Social Services (MDSS) was developing purchase of services contracts requiring performance objectives related to number of program successes at time of program completion, placement status of the client after program completion, and client length of stay in agency programs. In addition, Boysville was being asked by MDSS to serve a more difficult client which required greater staff skills. Agency leadership recognized that to function effectively and efficiently under these changing conditions required a new approach to management decision making.

These organizational changes and problems suggested the need for a new management information, practice decision making and program evaluation system at Boysville (BOMIS). Pressures from external accountability, funding, and accrediting systems reinforced this need (Grasso, 1992).

The unique approach to service delivery and the information system that developed in response to these conditions are the topics of this book. The following outlines the organization of the book and our method for presenting the material.

ORGANIZATION OF THE BOOK

Our strategy for articulating the necessary components of this integrative model involves the description of the underlying theoretical principles, design, implementation, and evaluation of an information-driven model of administration, training, supervision, and direct practice at Boysville. In addition, we offer examples of the multiple uses of the Boysville Management Information, Program Evaluation, and Practice Decision Making System (BOMIS), both internal to the organization and external.

The first article presents a review of the organizational literature which highlights a number of theoretical issues and organizational conflicts that must be taken into account if we are to succeed in developing an integrative system. More specifically, it discusses the conflicts generated by the introduction of research and information technologies into social service agencies and the potential contribution of these technologies to organizational performance.

The articles that follow are divided into three sections. The first section describes the underlying theoretical assumptions of the Boysville system and the organizational structures and processes that translate these assumptions into practice. The articles in this section are largely written by Boysville research staff.

The second section illustrates the programmatic uses of information provided by BOMIS. The articles in this section are written primarily by Boysville practice and administrative staff.

The final section, written by members of Boysville's National Research Advisory Committee, illustrates how BOMIS data can serve internal organizational purposes as well as reflect on broader issues in the field.

More generally, it is the intent of this special collection of *Child &*

Youth Services to present the reader with a case example of an innovative, agency-sponsored effort to create an organizational culture and structure that combines "state of the art" information technology and empirically-based, client-oriented practice. A number of these topics were discussed in some detail in Dr. Grasso's Disertation (Grasso, 1989).

REFERENCES

Briar, S. (1980). Toward the integration of practice and research. In D. Fanshel (Ed.), *The future of social work research*. NASW, 31-37.

Caputo, R. (1988). *Management and information systems in human services: Implications for the distribution of authority and decision making*. New York: Hawthorne Press.

Clark, D. L. (1985). Emerging paradigms in organizational theory and research. In Y. S. Lincoln (Ed.), *Organizational theory and inquiry: The paradigm shift*. Beverly Hills, CA: Sage Publications Inc.

Dickson, D. N. (1983). Using logical techniques for making better decisions. *Harvard Business Review*. New York: John Wiley & Sons.

Dunham, A. (1939). The administration of social agencies. *Social work yearbook*. New York: Russell Sage Foundation.

Etzioni, A. (1960). Two approaches to organization analysis: A critique and a suggestion. *Administrative Quarterly, 5*, 257-278.

Etzioni, A. (1964). *Modern organizations*. Englewood Cliffs, N.J.: Prentice-Hall, Inc.

Fabricant, M. (1985). The industrialization of social work. *Social Work, 30*, 389-395.

Grasso, A. (1992) Information Utilization: A decade of practice. In A. Grasso & I. Epstein (Eds.) Research Utilization in the Social Services: Innovations for practice and administration. New York: The Haworth Press, Inc.

Grasso, A. (1989) Integrating Management Information and Progress Evaluation at Boysville of Michigan. New York: Hunter College School of Social Work.

Grasso, A., & Epstein, I. (1987). Management by measurement: Organizational dilemmas and opportunities. *Administration in Social Work, 11*, 89-100.

Gruber, M. (1974). Total administration. *Social Work, 19*, 625-636.

Handy, C. (1976). *Understanding organizations*. New York: Penguin.

Henderson, J. (1986). Emerging trends and issues in decision support systems and related technologies: Implications for organizations. In G. R. Geiss & N. Viswanathan (Eds.), *The human edge: Information technology and helping people*. New York: The Haworth Press, Inc.

Katz, D., & Kahn, R. (1966). *The social psychology of organizations*. New York, Wiley.

Katz, D. & Kahn, R. (1978). *The social psychology of organizations*. 2nd Ed. New York: Wiley.

Lincoln, Y. S. (1985). Introduction. In Y. S. Lincoln (Ed.), *Organizational theory and inquiry: The paradigm shift*. Beverly Hills, CA: Sage Publications, Inc.

Patti, R. (1983). *Social welfare administration.* Englewood Cliffs, N.J.: Prentice-Hall, Inc.

Patti, R. (1985). In search of a purpose in social welfare administration. *Administration in Social Work, 9,* 1-14.

Patti, R., & Austin, M. (1977). Socializing the direct-service practitioner in ways of supervisory management. *Administration in Social Work, 1,* 273-80.

Perrow, C. (1974). The analysis of goals in complex organizations. In Y. Hasenfeld & R. A. English (Eds.), *Human service organizations.* Ann Arbor: University of Michigan Press, 214-229.

Rapp, C. A., & Poertner, J. (1987). Moving clients center stage through the use of client outcomes. *Administration in Social Work, 11,* 89-100.

Rothman, J. (1974). *Planning and organizing for social change.* New York: Columbia University Press, 531-576.

Tratner, W. (1979). *From poor law to welfare state,* 2nd Edition. New York: Free Press, Macmillan Publishing Company.

SECTION ONE

Theoretical Requirements for Successful Integration of Information Technology in Human Service Agencies

Anthony J. Grasso
Irwin Epstein

ABSTRACT. The relevant literature describes several obstacles to the integration of information technology and social work practice at each organizational level. This paper reviews that literature and describes its relevance to the design of the Boysville information system (BOMIS). More generally, it identifies the elements necessary for the design and implementation of an integrative model of information utilization for social service agencies.

The literature concerning models of social agency administration, the role of research and information technology in social service agencies, and

Anthony J. Grasso is Director, School of Social Work, University of Nevada at Las Vegas, 4505 Maryland Parkway, Las Vegas, NV 89154-5032. Irwin Epstein is affiliated with the School of Social Work, Hunter College, City University of New York, 129 East 79th Street, New York, NY 10021. Portions of this paper have previously been published in Administration in Social Work, 1987. The Haworth Press, Inc.

[Haworth co-indexing entry note]: "Theoretical Requirements for Successful Integration of Information Technology in Human Service Agencies." Grasso, Anthony J., and Irwin Epstein. Co-published simultaneously in *Child & Youth Services,* (The Haworth Press, Inc.) Vol. 16, No. 1, 1993, pp. 17-32; and: *Information Systems in Child, Youth, and Family Agencies: Planning, Implementation, and Service Enhancement* (ed: Anthony J. Grasso, and Irwin Epstein) The Haworth Press, Inc., 1993, pp. 17-32. Multiple copies of this article/chapter may be purchased from The Haworth Document Delivery Center. Call 1-800-3-HAWORTH (1-800-342-9678) between 9:00 - 5:00 (EST) and ask for DOCUMENT DELIVERY CENTER.

17

the integration of these with direct service delivery suggests a number of problems related to organizational performance. Associated with these problems are a series of conflicts in application that must be addressed if an integrated model is to be successful. These include:

1. conflicts between external accountability requirements and internal organizational needs;
2. conflicts generated within the organization based on the role-obligations associated with different positions in the organizational hierarchy;
3. conflicts associated with the introduction and ongoing utilization of computers in social service agencies; and
4. conflicts among various models of research and research utilization in social service agencies.

This introductory paper reviews the literature pertaining to these conflicts and their implications for organizational performance. More broadly, it serves as a theoretical backdrop for describing the Boysville information system and its multiple uses. Ultimately, it articulates the elements necessary for design and implementation of an integrative model of information utilization for social service agencies.

ORGANIZATIONAL PERFORMANCE IN THEORY AND PRACTICE

Organizational performance issues are some of the knottiest problems facing social service administrators. These problems are both theoretical and practical. The latter are discussed in a subsequent section of this paper which deals with practice conflicts within organizations. However, the theoretical aspects of these problems must first be addressed if an effective integrative model of administrative practice is to be achieved. In this first section of the paper, we present the theoretical aspects of the problem and show how an integrated model of information utilization and multilevel practice attempts to address them.

THEORETICAL ISSUES

The issue of organizational performance was first approached systematically in the organizational theory literature by Frederick Taylor (1911).

He proposed that by systematic observation and measurement any job could be broken down into a set of simple physical tasks. To accomplish this, he conducted time and motion studies of various menial jobs and empirically determined which series of tasks performed in which order produced the most efficient and effective result.

It is important to point out, however, that Taylor did not intend by this approach to educate the worker to be a better employee through the understanding of scientific management principles. Instead, Scientific Management education was reserved for the manager. Hence, for Taylor, the problem of organizational performance was not linked to the line workers' ignorance of the most productive way of working, but rather to the knowledge deficits of managers. As Taylor put it:

> And yet these foremen and superintendents know, better than anyone else, that their skill falls short of the combined knowledge and dexterity of all the workmen under them. The most experienced managers therefore frankly place before their workmen the problem of doing the work in the best and most economical way. (1911, pp. 32-33)

Ultimately, Taylor was trying to address the problem of organizational performance by increasing management's control over line workers, using scientific principles and empirical research to do so. In this regard, his working assumptions were:

1. Man is only interested in money and will by nature underwork;
2. All work can be broken into simple parts so that through routine one can gain efficiency; and
3. The simpler the job, the less dependent an organization is on workers since replacements can easily be found and trained.

Given these basic assumptions about work, workers, and organizations, Taylor used an empirical, research-based approach to reinforce the control of work by management as the way to improve organizational performance. As Vroom and Jago (1988) observed:

> Taylor's scientific management undoubtedly re-established management control in the American corporation. (p. 11)

After Taylor, other schools of management evolved. Most influential among these were the Human Relations motivational theorists, whose theoretical approach was a reaction against the dehumanization of the worker inherent in Scientific Management theory. Instead of seeing workers as individual extensions of machines, Human Relations theorists emphasized the social nature of work and asserted that worker participation in decisions was an important determinant of productivity. This model fit more closely with social work values than did Scientific Management and was adopted as the major theoretical approach to administration within social work (Patti, 1985).

However, an unresolved problem with this model of management was that it never adequately demonstrated that a positive relationship between worker satisfaction and worker performance exists (Brayfield & Crockett, 1955; Herzberg, Mausner, Peterson & Capwell, 1957; Kahn, 1960; Opsahl & Dunnette, 1966; Smith & Cranny, 1968; Vroom, 1964). Nevertheless, all of the current participatory approaches to management, such as quality circles, are an outgrowth of Human Relations theory and as such are more syntonic with social work values.

Despite the inroads made by Human Relations theory and its practice applications in social work agencies, Scientific Management still dominates American industrial management because, at the very least, Scientific Management has demonstrated its ability to improve organizational efficiency. Other models of organization have failed notably on this crucial dimension. As Braverman (1974) noted:

> It is impossible to overestimate the importance of the scientific management movement in the shaping of the modern corporation and indeed all institutions of capitalistic society which carry on labor processes. The popular notions that Taylorism has been superseded by later schools of industrial psychology or human relations . . . represent a woeful misreading of the actual dynamics of the development of management. (pp. 86-87)

In contrast with the corporate experience, attempts to apply Scientific Management techniques to social work organizations have encountered resistance from those who emphasize the "softer" more humanistic character of social work practice (Fabricant, 1985; Gruber, 1974). These writers assert the existence of a basic value conflict in the way social work administrators and proponents of Scientific Management view the worker and work. Thus, Scientific Management has been resisted by social workers because it implies that the craft or art of social work practice can be reduced to a set of discrete tasks that can be aggregated in such a way as to produce a social work automaton. This, coupled with the assumption of worker untrustworthiness, has resulted in the wholesale condemnation of the Scientific Management approach by social work theoreticians and administrators.

Unfortunately, in doing so, they have also rejected an aspect of the Scientific Management approach which is potentially compatible with social work values and, at the same time, likely to improve organizational performance. What Scientific Management can teach us is how we can improve organizational efficiency and effectiveness by the strategic use of information relevant to the performance of each individual worker. To do this, however, the useful principles of Scientific Management must be sensitively accomodated to social work values and agency-based practice models.

For example, although Taylor emphasized the way in which information empowers the manager to control the worker, the integrative model of information utilization articulated by Grasso and Epstein (1987), implemented at Boysville, and illustrated in this volume suggests that much the same information be given to the direct service worker, to empower her/him with the ability to improve practice decisions. To achieve this, the character of information provided to the line worker must be tailored to the information needs and practice paradigms employed by the worker.

In its original form, then, the Scientific Management approach could not be successful in improving organizational performance in human service agencies because its primary emphasis was on promoting management control. Seen from a different vantage point, however, Scientific Management is an empirically-based, information-driven, decision making approach which has the potential to empower workers and to improve performance at every organizational level. Drawing upon this proposition, a successful integrative practice model for social work such as the one developed at Boysville can integrate organizational performance with social work values through the empowerment of line workers by providing them with information to improve their individual performance. If this model is implemented at all organizational levels, it will aggregate to improve overall organizational performance.

CONFLICTS BETWEEN ACCOUNTABILITY REQUIREMENTS AND INTERNAL ORGANIZATIONAL NEEDS

Although social workers have resisted the incursions of Scientific Management and organizational sociologists have warned us against over-reliance on effectiveness models (Etzioni, 1964; Hasenfeld, 1983), the accountability movement, the advent of the computer, and the resort to business administration techniques in times of scarcity, have led human service organizations and their funding sources to place great emphasis on statistical measurement of effort, effectiveness and efficiency. For agencies and programs, life and death decisions are often based on statistical indicators such as number of client contacts, number of units of service delivered, number of closed cases, average length of stay, and the like (Bielawski & Epstein, 1984; Conrad, 1985).

This emphasis on quantitative measures of effectiveness and efficiency has resulted in a number of different types of conflicts and goal displacements inside human service organizations. So, for example, in discussing the phenomenon of over-measurement, Etzioni (1964) points out that:

> Frequent measuring can distort . . . organizational efforts because as a rule, some aspects of its output are more measurable than others. Frequent measuring tends to encourage overproduction of measurable items and neglect less measurable ones. (p. 9)

To illustrate this point, Conrad (1985) has shown that the Program Assessment System (PAS) applied to New York City foster care workers, encourages them to put more emphasis on accomplishing a certain number of parental visits, for example, or the placing of a child in an adoptive home by the required date, rather than the way it is accomplished. At the administrative level she shows how the same measurement system puts pressure on foster care administrators to "displace the goal of family reunification because of the very procedures devised to achieve this goal" (p. 642).

Elsewhere, Hasenfeld (1983) has warned of "the tendency by the organization to reify these measures as true indicators of effectiveness." In doing so, "the organization allocates its resources and concentrates its efforts to score well on these criteria, despite their real limitations" (p. 212). Whether or not the criteria are inherently valid, organizations may seek clients that most approximate "output criteria" at intake (Dale, 1984). If they cannot control intake, programs may jettison unpromising clients before they can show up as indicators of program failure (Lerman, 1968). Finally, Walker (1972) has talked about the "strain towards falsification" (p. 47), whereby, staff are pressured to lie with statistics in order to make their programs and themselves look good in the eyes of external evaluators and internal superiors.

The causes of these dysfunctions are, among others, "the multiplicity and ambiguity of organizational goals, the indeterminacy of the service technologies, and the inherent difficulties in observing and measuring human attributes," such as client change (Hasenfeld, 1983, p. 10-11). Moreover, in contrast with industrial organizations where the work orientations of staff are more instrumental and focused upon outputs, workers in human service organizations tend to stress professional autonomy, humanistic rather than instrumental objectives, and professional "process" as opposed to "outcomes" (Kouzes & Mico, 1979). Nevertheless, and despite the resistances described above, it is probably safe to predict that effectiveness models and statistical assessment of organizational and worker performance are here to stay.

More specifically, in social agencies, the imposition of effectiveness models by funding sources has led program administrators to measure performance in terms of number counts of staff activity (e.g., client contact, services provided, etc.), client outputs (e.g., cases closed, type of program completion, satisfaction with service, etc.), and client outcomes (e.g., recidivism, post-treatment adjustment, etc.). Students of human service organizations have suggested, however, that the common administrative practice of measuring success in order to meet external accountability requirements often conflicts with internal program needs and the needs of clients. Thus, in discussing PAS, Conrad (1985) comments:

> Whether the primary motivating force behind these . . . [measures] is to improve services or reduce costs, their imposition has created as many problems as it has resolved. Thus, the sheer number and complexity of these requirements pose an enormous problem for administrators, supervisors, and workers alike. (p. 640)

Despite their common administrative origin, these conflicts get played out in different ways at different program levels within the organization. This is because each level is likely to have a different set of criteria for assessing effectiveness and efficiency, different organizational loyalties, different informational needs and different central tasks. On this latter point, Patti (1983) remarks:

> While there are essential similarities this should not obscure the fact that the relative emphasis given to tasks and thus the activity configurations of management varies significantly with the organizational level in which the practice occurs. (p. 43)

The increasing development of external accountability systems has magnified the conflicts regarding organizational performance. Irrespective of the type of agency and level of analysis, external accountability efforts assume that staff should be held "accountable for specific service outputs and . . . rewarded according to their ability to attain them" (Hasenfeld, 1983, p. 174). A successful integrative model of information utilization for social work must satisfy external accountability requirements, yet at the same time support and reward line level practitioners for the best possible work with their clients.

CONFLICTS ASSOCIATED WITH DIFFERENCES
IN THE ORGANIZATIONAL HIERARCHY

In studying human service organizational hierarchies, Patti (1983) has identified four levels for analysis: the executive management level; the program management level; the supervisory management level; and the program staff level. The challenge of developing an integrative administrative model for social work has problematic implications for each of the different program levels inside the agency. In small agencies, a number of different problems simultaneously confront the same individuals (i.e., those with multiple roles and multiple responsibilities). In large, highly differentiated agencies, these same dilemmas and conflicts confront different staff levels in singular ways and cause conflicts between staff levels.

Beginning at the program staff (line) level, individuals have a primary obligation to deliver quality service to agency clients. Workers at this lowest level in the hierarchy must mediate the conflicts between two external sets of demands, those of the client for more service and those of accountability sources for greater efficiency. The latter demands are expressed through their supervisors.

The supervisory level in the organization is the first point in the organizational structure where position in the hierarchy places a strain on role occupant from above and from below the organization. Because of their clinical training and program staff origins, the ideological commitment of supervisors is more likely to be with the preservation and implementation of the professional technology than with organizational maintenance. Because of this, supervisors often identify with the direct service professionals in an organization rather than with those in higher levels of administration.

Social work supervision is particularly problematic because it involves overseeing the implementation of "soft," people-changing technologies that have not as yet been demonstrated to have a clear cause-and-effect relationship. Nevertheless, supervisors are ultimately responsible for the outcomes or performance of the staff below them. Consequently, role conflict for social work supervisors results from being held responsible for service effects without having the information necessary to properly teach, monitor and evaluate line worker interventions with clients.

Despite their commitment to direct service concerns, their hierarchical positions place supervisors in a constant struggle with line workers over the control of the treatment process. Line workers often seek total autonomy. Supervisors seek accountability, even if only to them. As the management process is formalized in the agency, accountability is often translated into activity counts of some kind (number of phone calls, number of client sessions conducted, etc.). Consequently, the service practitioner often complains that paperwork gets in the way of helping clients while supervisors are required to ask for completed reports and high scores on activity measures.

The program management level in the organization is more often committed to organizational maintenance than to the preservation of professional autonomy. Although committed to the primary value of accountability, middle managers who are trained as social workers have found it problematic responding to models of accountability developed in the corporate sector. These models place middle-level managers in conflict with supervisors. The latter emphasize the utilization of professional skills, while the former are primarily responsible to report and control. In addition, the middle-level manager is faced with the problem of distinguishing between ritualized compliance and really high quality work. Often identifying with business or corporate models of administration, social workers at this level in the organization have a more tenuous identification with the field of social services than their subordinates. Instead, they sometimes see themselves as corporate managers.

Corporate identification notwithstanding, the inexactness of human service technology severely limits the applicability of corporate management information systems and administrative models in human services. Frustration at the middle-management level is associated with a lack of appropriate assessment approaches that provide for accountability but also support human service management and administration.

The executive level in the organization is the level where role incumbents are more concerned with general operations than with the day-to-day management of the organization. In relation to service delivery, their primary concern is the production of demonstrable results as opposed to the conduct of professional process. The executive staff level may experience conflict in communicating to the external environment as they find themselves defending the good work their organization does, while at the same time dealing with information from middle level-managers about far from perfect program outcomes.

These hierarchical differences have been discussed extensively in the social work literature dealing with the purported conflict between bureaucratic and professional authority (Scott, 1965; Aiken & Hage, 1968). These discussions generally assume that those higher in the organizational structure will be more committed to bureaucratic authority while those lower in the hierarchy will emphasize professional autonomy. Empirical studies of this issue have demonstrated, however, that social workers at all organizational levels struggle to reconcile conflicting commitments to client need, professional values, and agency accountability (Billingsley, 1964; Epstein & Conrad, 1978; Reeser & Epstein, 1990).

With regard to the use of information in the agency, these problems are often translated into a conflict over qualitative versus quantitative measures of worker performance. For direct service workers, effectiveness is not reducible to quantitative measures of numbers of client contacts or cases closed, but instead relates to whether clients experienced a qualitative improvement in a painful circumstance. For such workers, number counts do not adequately reflect what they do or accomplish. On the other hand, because of accountability pressures and the appropriate concern of administrators to describe program accomplishments externally, administrators emphasize aggregate, quantitative measures of program performance.

With administration pressing for performance criteria, however, a major epistemological and empirical problem emerges. More specifically, emphasis on quantitative measures of client contacts reflects an assumption about the relationship between quantification of intervention activity and its effect. This implicit proposition has never been tested. Even if such a correlation were to exist, questions about causation are likely to remain unanswered (Kadushin, 1976; Smith, 1976).

Nonetheless, as a consequence of this pressure for quantification, clinical practitioners come to resent evaluative systems because they do not take into account the difficulty of a case or level of skill required to achieve desired outcomes. Despite their resistance to them, however, direct service workers see these measurement systems increasingly being used by administration for individual performance evaluation as well as for program evaluation.

In considering this problem, Weissman (1977) asserts that evaluation must provide operating staff with direct information not only about their job performance, but, much more significantly, about how to improve their work. He states that if human service professionals are merely held accountable for results, but not given the kind of informational help to improve their performance, misinformation about success may be introduced into the system, or, as Merton (1952) pointed out, overconformity and excessive caution in action may result. Weissman further suggests that program evaluation must be separated from individual staff evaluation in order to reduce the defensive perception by staff that they, rather than their programs, are being evaluated.

Clearly, an effective, integrative model of social work administration and information utilization must successfully mediate the conflicts between different organizational levels to support high quality performance at each level and to reduce conflicts between them. In addition, it must promote staff learning and professional growth at each level.

CONFLICT ASSOCIATED WITH THE INTRODUCTION OF COMPUTERS

The introduction of computer technology into a social work agency presents several dilemmas and conflicts. The first conflict involves the allocation of resources within an organization. Since practitioners focus primarily on individual client needs, while organizations have limited resources, the introduction of computers creates a perceived and real conflict over scarce resources among social work agency staff.

In this context, direct service practitioners often feel that money could better be spent on serving individual client needs. Administration, however, who view computers as promoting accountability and efficiency are more likely to be committed to developing an information system. As a result, administrators are often more willing and certainly more able, to free limited resources for development and purchase of computer hardware and software than their clinical staff might like.

In addition, the implementation of computerized information systems place more demands on line staff who now have to take time away from serving individual clients to fill out forms. This resource conflict is fairly universal in that most organizations are not able to hire additional staff or reduce work loads.

Computers also promote a "systemic" approach to program design and implementation. For direct service workers steeped in a "case-by-case" approach to practice that emphasizes the uniqueness of each client, such a systemic approach presents additional value conflicts.

Another conflict involves the need for specific, measurable, quantitative information that can be efficiently entered into the computer, stored and retrieved in quantitative report formats. Since human service organizations do not possess exact technologies or conceptualize their effects in measurable terms, the requirement of this kind of information from human service programs is often problematic. The introduction of the computer exacerbates these conflicts by compelling practitioners to think in terms of measurable objectives and empirically-based decision making. More often than not, practitioners respond negatively to this pressure.

Finally, the agency's introduction of a computerized information system necessitates integrating a new technology into social work practice along with a new professional orientation which, to a certain extent, may provide an advantage in the competition for the administration's time, energy, and resource allocation. To the extent that this new technology promotes organizational structures that emphasize performance and accountability, it creates a profound power shift within the organization; a new locus of power has control over information as well as agency capital resources. In addition, it provides those at the upper reaches of the organization with more information concerning the activity of staff at lower levels than they had in the past. Although administrators may view this positively, this change may prove dysfunctional when line staff are not also empowered with the information required to improve their skills and performance.

While they are likely to express themselves in computer terms, these dysfunctions have roots in basic human learning theory. They also have broad and profound implications for social work practice. Thus, for individuals to learn and create, they must be free to doubt. When pressured by administration to perform better but denied the resources to do so, workers no longer feel that freedom. As a result, computerization may put pressure on staff to conceal their practice problems and hide their professional doubts from themselves as well as peers and superiors. This inhibits professional growth and performance improvement.

An effective, integrative model of information utilization for social work must incorporate computer technology. It must, at the same time, minimize potential dysfunction by empowering direct service workers with practice-relevant information for improving performance.

CONFLICTS ASSOCIATED WITH DIFFERENT MODELS OF RESEARCH AND RESEARCH UTILIZATION

Discussions of the failure to incorporate research into social work practice parallel problems associated with promoting computerization and information utilization in social work agencies. In these discussions, emphasis is placed on conflicting attitudes of practitioners and researchers or conflicting allegiances of agency-based social workers and academically-oriented researchers.

So, for example, Briar (1980) has explained the lack of integration of practice and research in light of the practitioner's inability to formulate, or resistance to formulating, practice interventions and treatment objectives in researchable terms. As he puts it:

> It appears to be a general principle in social work never to use a specifically descriptive term if a more abstract one is available. The nearer terms get to operational or behavioral specificity, the more social workers turn away from them. (p. 33)

In a less cynical and more even-handed discussion of practitioner and researcher attitudes, Rothman (1974) locates the problem in interaction between practitioner and researcher. He comments:

> Different styles and modes of thinking divide the two types (practitioner/researcher) which makes communication difficult and utilization of each other's contributions and products problematic. There exists formidable social distance characterized by mistrust, differing outlooks and ostensibly contrasting goals which, in the past, has inhibited fuller articulation between social scientists and social practitioners. (p. 545)

Rather than anti-research attitudes, Gordon (1984) posits blame on practitioners' lack of skill in deriving practice applications from research studies as one of the central points in the conflict. Lewis (1980), on the other hand, is critical of conceptual and methodological paradigms brought by academic researchers to the study of practice. Thus, he suggests:

> It is the design of research including its implementation and the form in which its findings are developed that one must locate the principle impediments to utilization. (p. 26)

In a continuing effort to address these problems of research design and implementation, Epstein and Tripodi (1977) favor using formative rather than summative evaluative research designs. They have developed conceptual frameworks and research strategies that link program level research to stages of program development and clinically-oriented research to stages of clinical intervention (Tripodi & Epstein, 1980).

Still other authors have located a problem of integration in research products themselves. Weiss (1972), for example, has noted that research findings are frequently not applicable to practice. Rothman (1974) suggests that findings, when applicable, still require too much translation for the practitioner to see them as useful. Seidl (1980) has commented on the failure of researchers to produce findings in a timely and usable form for practitioners.

A final set of problems involves likely structural and physical locations of researcher and practitioner. Thus, Bushnell and O'Brien (1979) have discussed several reasons why university-based research is not likely to be applied by practitioners. Arguing instead for the location of research at the agency, Seidl (1980) notes:

> If research is to be timely and space specific, and to deal in practitioner's language with relevant and researchable variables, it must be conducted where direct practice is carried out. (p. 60)

Even when research is agency-based, its applicability to practice can vary depending upon the model of research employed. Thus, Kirk (1979) has discussed the utilization pros and cons of three models of agency-based research articulated by Havelock (1969):

> The R&D models emphasized the role of the research and development and the rational planning of diffusion efforts but it pays little attention to the role of the consumer of knowledge. The social interaction model perspective carefully documents the importance of social networks and understanding the flow of knowledge and utilization through a user system, however, it fails to articulate the linkage between the producer and users of knowledge. The problem solver model directs attention to the psychological conditions under which a new knowledge may be sought out and used by consumers but it over-emphasizes the extent to which consumers are capable of generating their own solution to problems. (p. 7)

Placing emphasis on the service consumer rather than the research consumer, Weissman (1977) advocates an agency-based evaluation system based on client perception and satisfaction. However, he points out that such a system will only succeed to the extent that service providers are committed to it and it provides timely and useful information.

The foregoing literature concerning research utilization suggests there is no single explanation for failure to incorporate research into our models of administrative practice. Nevertheless, programs designed to promote practice utilization of computerized information and research must address staff attitudes, staff utilization skills, timeliness and applicability of the research products, location and orientation of researchers, and model of research employed. An effective, integrative model of information utilization for social work agencies must do all of the above.

REFERENCES

Aiken, M., & Hage, J. (1968). Organizational interdependence and interorganizational structure. *American Sociological Review, 33*, 912-930.

Bielawski, B., & Epstein, I. (1984). Assessing program stagnazation: An extension of the differential evaluation model. *Administration in Social Work, 8*, 13-23.

Billingsley, A. (1964). Bureaucratic and professional orientation patterns in social casework. *Social Service Review, 4*, 400-07.

Braverman, H. (1974). *Labor and monopoly capital: The degradation of work in the twentieth century.* New York: Monthly Review Press.

Brayfield, A. H., & Crockett, W. H. (1955). Employee attitudes and employee performance. *Psychological Bulletin, 52*, 396-424.

Briar, S. (1980). Toward the integration of practice and research. In D. Fanshel (Ed.), *Future of social work research.* NASW, 31-37.

Bushnell, J. L., & O'Brien, G. M. (1979). Strategies and tactics for increasing research production and utilization in social work education. In A. Rubin & A. Rosenblatt (Eds.), *Sourcebook on research utilization.* New York: Council on Social Work Education, 169-188.

Conrad, K. (1985). Promoting quality of care: The role of the compliance director. *Child Welfare, 64*, 639-649.

Dale, N. (1984). The new foster care system: A procrustean bed. *The Children's Village Bulletin, 4.*

Epstein, I., & Conrad, K. (1978). The empirical limits of social work professionalization. In R. C. Sarri & Y. Hasenfeld, (Eds.), *The management of human services.* New York: Columbia University Press, 163-183.

Epstein, I., & Tripodi, T. (1977). *Research techniques for program planning, monitoring and evaluation.* New York: Columbia University Press.

Etzioni, A. (1964). *Modern organizations.* Englewood Cliffs, N.J.: Prentice-Hall, Inc.

Fabricant, M. (1985). The industrialization of social work. *Social Work, 30*, 389-395.

Gordon, J. E. (1984). Creating research based practice principles: A model. *Social Work Research and Abstracts*, 3-6.

Grasso, A., & Epstein, I. (1987). Management by measurement: Organizational dilemmas and opportunities. *Administration in Social Work, 11*, 89-100.

Gruber M. (1974). Total administration. *Social Work, 19*, 625-636.

Hasenfeld, Y. (1983). *Human service organizations.* Englewood Cliffs, N.J.: Prentice-Hall, Inc.

Havelock, R. G. (1969). *Planning for innovations: Through dissemination and utilization of knowledge.* Ann Arbor, Michigan: Institute for Social Research.

Herzberg, F., Mausner, B., Peterson, R. O., & Capwell, D. F. (1957). *Job attitudes: Review of research and opinion.* Pittsburgh: Psychological Service of Pittsburgh.

Kadushin, A. (1976). Children in foster families and institutions. In H. Maas

(Ed.), *Social service research: Review of studies.* Washington, D.C.: NASW, 90-148.

Kahn, R. L. (1960). Productivity and job satisfaction. *Personnel Psychology, 13,* 275-287.

Kirk, S. (1979). Understanding research utilization in social work. In A. Rubin & A. Rosenblatt (Eds.), *Sourcebook on research utilization.* New York: Council on Social Work Education, 132-140.

Kouzes, J., & Mico, P. (1979). Domain theory. *Journal of Applied Science.*

Lerman, P. (1968). Evaluative studies of institutions for delinquents: Implications for research and social policy. *Social Work, 13,* 55-64.

Lewis, H. (1980). Toward a planned approach in social work research. In D. Fanshel (Ed.), *Future of social work research.* New York: NASW, 19-28.

Merton, R. (1952). Bureaucratic structure and personality. In R. Merton, A. Gray, B. Hackey, & H. Salvin (Eds.), *Reader in bureaucracy.* Glencoe, Ill: The Free Press, 366.

Opsahl, R. L., & Dunnette, M. D. (1966). The role of financial compensation in industrial motivation. *Psychological Bulletin, 66,* 94-118.

Patti, R. (1983). *Social welfare administration.* Englewood Cliffs, N.J.: Prentice-Hall, Inc.

Patti, R. (1985). In search of a purpose in social welfare administration. *Administration in Social Work, 9,* 1-14.

Reeser, L. C., & Epstein, I. (1990). *Professionalization and activism in social work: The 60's, the 80's and the future.* New York: Columbia University Press.

Rothman, J. (1974). *Planning and organizing for social change.* New York: Columbia University Press, 531-576.

Scott, R. (1965). Reactions to supervision in a heteronomous professional organization. *Administrative Science Quarterly, 10,* 65-81.

Seidl, F. (1980). Making research relevant for practitioners. In D. Fanshel (Ed.), *Future of social work research.* New York: NASW, 53-62.

Smith, M. (1976). A question about parental visiting and foster care. *Social Service Review, 50,* 525-526.

Smith, P. C., & Cranny, C. J. (1968). Psychology of men at work. *Annual Review of Psychology, 19,* 467-496.

Taylor, F. W. (1911). *Scientific management.* New York: Harper & Bros.

Tripodi, T., & Epstein, I. (1980). *Research techniques for clinical social work.* New York: Columbia University Press.

Vroom, V. H. (1964). *Work and motivation.* New York: Wiley.

Vroom, V. H., & Jago A. G. (1988). *The new leadership.* Englewood Cliffs, N.J.: Prentice-Hall, Inc.

Walker, R. (1972). The ninth panacea: Program evaluation. *Evaluation, 1,* 45-53.

Weiss, C. (1972). *Evaluating action programs: Readings in social action and education.* Boston: Allyn & Bacon, 10-11.

Weissman, E. (1977). Clients, staff, and researchers: Their role in management information systems. *Administration in Social Work, 1,* 43-51.

BOMIS:
A Management Information System
for Children and Youth Service Providers

Stephen A. Kapp
Anthony J. Grasso

ABSTRACT. Designers of information systems often fail to take into account the different, and at times, conflicting information needs of social workers who function at different organizational levels. This paper articulates a set of information system design principles which rest on the assumption that, in order to be most useful, the system must meet the unique information needs of decision makers at each level. Based upon these principles and their underlying assumption, this paper provides an overview of the structure, content, and uses of Boysville's information system (BOMIS).

If properly conceptualized, packaged, and fed back, management information system data have multiple uses and can contribute to effective decision making at all organizational levels. Based upon this premise,

Stephen A. Kapp is affiliated with Boysville of Michigan, 8744 Clinton-Macon Road, Clinton, MI 49236. Anthony J. Grasso is Director, School of Social Work, University of Nevada at Las Vegas, 4505 Maryland Parkway, Las Vegas, NV 89154-5032.

[Haworth co-indexing entry note]: "BOMIS: A Management Information System for Children and Youth Service Providers." Kapp, Stephen A., and Anthony J. Grasso. Co-published simultaneously in *Child & Youth Services*, (The Haworth Press, Inc.) Vol. 16, No. 1, 1993, pp. 33-47; and: *Information Systems in Child, Youth, and Family Agencies: Planning, Implementation, and Service Enhancement* (ed: Anthony J. Grasso, and Irwin Epstein) The Haworth Press, Inc., 1993, pp. 33-47. Multiple copies of this article/chapter may be purchased from The Haworth Document Delivery Center. Call 1-800-3-HAWORTH (1-800-342-9678) between 9:00 - 5:00 (EST) and ask for DOCUMENT DELIVERY CENTER.

Grasso and Epstein (1987) have conceived of four organizational strata of potential information users: Line Service Workers, Supervisors, Program Managers, and Executives. They go on to point out, however, that differing and sometimes conflicting informational needs at different organizational levels pose a challenge for MIS professionals. They suggest that information systems are often inadequate because designers fail to attend to these differences and conflicts. Often in responding to these conflicts, designers compromise the information needs of direct service practitioners in favor of the accountability-oriented information needs of program managers and administrators.

There are many causes of this fundamental design error. One is that academic researchers, who have frequently been responsible for designing information systems, have inadequate knowledge of or interest in treatment technologies (Reid, 1980). Another is the understandable emphasis that program managers and administrators, who contract with MIS designers, place on accountability needs (Grasso & Epstein, 1987). In some organizations, the result of overemphasis on accountability information is goal displacement (Conrad, 1985; Hasenfeld, 1983). In these organizations, direct service staff are burdened with extensive data collection responsibilities but benefit little from the information collected (Hoshino, 1982). As a result, the quality and accuracy of this information is often questionable (Walker, 1972).

In responding to this dilemma, different strategies have been suggested for ensuring that information systems provide clinically useful information feedback to treatment staff in return for their data-collection efforts. One approach is to create systems designs and choose interactive computer hardware and software that maximizes the likelihood of integrating administrative and clinical information (Mutschler & Hasenfeld, 1986). Another, emphasizing single-subject methodology, suggests a more active role for direct service practitioners in designing single case evaluation systems (Blythe & Briar, 1985).

Typically, however, discussions of information systems design for the human services have presented unintegrated and undifferentiated models for "total" systems (Bronson, Pelz, & Trzcinski, 1988), or highly specific information systems that serve the decisional needs of one organizational group while ignoring the other groups in the agency (Caputo, 1988). By contrast, Grasso and Epstein's (1987) approach to systems design can best be described as an utilization-driven design that integrates clinical, supervisory, and administrative information, but begins with the information needs of the direct service practitioner.

Their model rests on the following principles (Grasso & Epstein, 1989):

1. Effective integration of the service technology and the accountability system of an agency requires that attention be given to actual as well as measured performance.
2. Effective integration of the service technology and the accountability system of an agency requires valid and reliable information from line staff.
3. Line staff will provide valid and reliable information to the degree that they receive, in return, information feedback that is timely and readily applicable to their practice (p. 87).

These design principles flow directly from a basic assumption that if management information systems are to be fully useful, they must provide useful information to all levels of the organization. In so saying, it is essential that the system meet the information needs of direct service practitioners who must gather the information in the first place. Finally, to achieve this end, clinically-relevant information must be further specified by the stage of client career in a program (Epstein & Grasso, 1987).

Based on the foregoing principles and assumptions, this paper describes the Boysville of Michigan Information System (BOMIS) currently used at the agency, and provides the data base for subsequent articles in this collection. The article offers an overview of the informational components of the system and the hardware and software utilized by it. It goes on to discuss the application of the foregoing principles in managing the current system as well as the design of new elements in the system. Finally, it describes the central role of the direct service practitioner in collecting and using information processed by BOMIS.

OVERVIEW OF THE INFORMATION SYSTEM

Original Components

Designed in 1983, the original components of BOMIS were fully operational by 1984. Since the treatment venue of the agency was, at the time, primarily residential, and the treamtent technology increasingly committed to a structural family therapy approach, BOMIS was designed to routinely collect family assessment information at different stages in the client's movement through the program. Information collected draws heavily on four family and adolescent assessment instruments developed by Olson, McCubbin et al. (1982) and two staff rating instruments which assess client behavior while in placement. This and other information is gathered at four discrete stages of a client's career in the agency–intake (input), intervention (throughput), program completion (output), and follow-up (outcome). At intake, information concerning client characteristics such as previous placements in other programs, seriousness of offense, family composition and standard demographic information (race, sex, etc.) is collected in addition to the previously mentioned diagnostic information. With these background and diagnostic data, agency staff are able to systematically assess clients who come to Boysville and develop client treatment plans.

At the intervention stage, BOMIS stores and analyzes information on worker/client interactions, critical incidents, staff rating of client behavior and client change. This information is used in conjunction with child and family instruments for modifying and improving treatment interventions and for some program management decisions at the supervisory level.

Upon program completion, BOMIS collects information on conditions at client termination. This includes data regarding success/failure, placement destination, completion of family work program as well as individual and family coping scores at time of termination. This information is used to determine whether individual clients and their families have achieved treatment goals and through aggregation makes possible individual worker, unit, and program level evaluation.

At the follow-up stage, information is gathered at three, twelve, and eighteen months after client termination. This information includes client placement status with the family, jail or other settings; educational status; employment status; and client/police contacts. This information allows Boysville to make inferences about program impact on clients after termination.

In addition to the foregoing data concerning client progress, BOMIS gathers information concerning staff activity on an individual worker and a unit basis. Using this information in conjunction with assessment measures, supervisors can provide more effective individual and group supervision and identify staff training needs. This information is aggregated and distributed in management-oriented reports concerning program performance and contract compliance. Finally, BOMIS provides executive staff with data which are used for assessing broad agency policy, influencing public policy external to the agency, and procuring additional funding.

After three years of system operation as described, it became clear that there was a need to increase the scope of data collection and potential for practitioner feedback as emerging client needs dictated. The educational and sexual abuse information systems outlined below represent additions to BOMIS based on more recently identified informational needs. Nonetheless, the same principles which governed the development of the original system were employed in the design of these new components.

Educational MIS

Observing the benefits that treatment staff were deriving from BOMIS, line educational staff requested expansion of the educational information system so as to lead to more effective decision making regarding clients' educational performance. This request led to the following enhancements.

At intake, additional information is collected concerning past educational history, describing previous educational settings, disciplinary problems, special education status, etc. Additionally, a complete psychological test (Wechsler, 1974), a classroom behavioral assessment (McCarney, 1985), as well as reading, math and written language achievement tests are administered (Woodcock & Johnson, 1977). This information improves educational staff's ability to systematically assess a client and to develop individualized educational plans in response to identified needs.

At the intervention stage, achievement tests and behavioral assessments are readministered for the purpose of assessing and improving educational interventions. This information is again collected at program completion allowing for fulfillment of contractual accountability requirements.

At the time of program completion, additional information is collected regarding the child's educational placement while at the facility, particularly special education services, tutoring, etc. Although some of this information had been previously collected manually, the addition of this component to BOMIS provided standardized information processing, data collection, and reporting protocols which are essential for agency-wide educational evaluation and training efforts.

Sexual Abuse MIS

As staff came to recognize the potential usefulness of BOMIS, they began to identify more information gaps in, and potential uses of, the system. Treatment staff, for example, focused on the incomplete sexual abuse histories of youths in placement. This informational need became apparent as discrepancies emerged between clinical impressions of clients by treatment staff and the remarkably low incidence of sexual abuse in client intake information and BOMIS reports. This apparent discrepancy between clinical observation of children in placement and intake data led to an extensive study of the case files (Epstein & Grasso, 1990).

Based upon data recorded in treatment files, the study found that incidence of youth involvement with sexual abuse prior to placement was probably at least three times higher than that reported in intake data. This new estimate led to the development of a major information collection and clinical training initiative targeted at equipping staff with specific skills for collecting sexual abuse information and addressing treatment needs of this previously underreported population.

Theoretical concepts and clinical tools employed in the training program (e.g., a sexual offender typology and a sexual abuse disclosure validation process) were then incorporated into data-collection instruments to be completed by treatment staff. In this new package, separate offender and victim instruments assess information about the last sexual abuse event, i.e., the specific behaviors involved, circumstances surrounding the event, sexual abuse history, etc. Another instrument focuses on the family's reaction to disclosure of the information and the family's role in the incident. A final instrument identifies progress toward the resolution of specific issues in the treatment process.

The new sexual abuse component of BOMIS is now utilized to enhance the clinical assessment, treatment and evaluation process for youths identified as sexual abuse victims and/or perpetrators. It provides concrete assessment tools that suggest specific treatment approaches, monitoring and evaluation measures.

Table 1 provides a schematic representation of the current informational components of BOMIS, stage at which information is collected, staff responsible for information collection, and focus of the information.

HARDWARE AND SOFTWARE

BOMIS was originally designed on the relational database Condor, but it has been recently rewritten in R-Base System V in order to take advantage of network capacity not offered with Condor. Graphics programs were written, as external procedures to the database, in Turbo-Pascal using Halo Graphics language. All other external routines, such as computation of complex family scores, are written in Turbo-Pascal using an R-Bridge utility function. The central storage and processing system is a Novell S with off-site direct access capability. Graphics are generated on an IBM XT 640 with a 20 meg hard disk drive and a Number Nine Revolution Graphics Board using a Data Products 8070 Colorgraphics printer. Report generation and statistical analysis is done on an IBM AT 1 meg with a 30 meg hard drive system. All data entry is done on IBM XTs, with 640K and 20 meg hard drives located at each of Boysville's 40 sites. The machines are also used for word processing and other functions by secretarial staff.

BOMIS is run by a research department that is made up of a Director of Research/MIS, who is accountable to the Director of the Boysville Institute, as well as an Assistant Director of Research, a Manager of MIS, a Research Assistant, a Computer Operator, 2 Computer Programmers and a Secretary. The Research Director is an MSW with a concentration and extensive post-master's degree experience in program evaluation. The Assistant Director is an MSW with a concentration in interpersonal practice and research. The Manager of MIS has a Bachelor's degree in Computer Science. The department is structurally linked to the Office of Clinical Staff Development by its relationship with the Boysville Institute. Beyond the formal linkage, a close working relationship between the two departments is cultivated since the use of research-based information for staff development and training is central to this design.

FLOW OF INFORMATION

Figure 1 illustrates the flow of information throughout the system. Data are collected by program staff administering survey instruments to youths and families. The information is entered and verified by the on-site secretaries and forwarded to evaluation staff in the research department for more complete verification and processing.

The Research Department also packages information to meet specialized consumer needs through specially designed and routinely generated reports. For example, treatment staff receive specific feedback on individual youths and families throughout placement in an easy-to-read graphic format. Supervisory staff receive single program summary reports of various types of process information, such as the number and types of staff/family contacts or the number of runaways from programs. The Management level receives the same information reported by program site in aggregated form. In addition, management level staff receive outcome information including success/failure rate and length of stay for program units. The executive staff receive outcome information organized at the level of the entire agency.

Another major use of this information is the statistical analysis of aggregate data to reflect issues that have relevance beyond the agency itself. Some of the articles that follow represent examples of this database being utilized to shed empirical light on practice, administrative, and policy questions. This information is shared through a department newsletter, and disseminated externally through books and articles in professional journals, conference presentations, workshops, and organizational consultations.

Table 1
System Instrumentation

	input	throughput	output	outcome
INTAKE (gt, y)	X			
FAMILY STRESS (fw, f)	X			
COPING SKILLS (gt, y)	X	X		
COPING SKILLS (fw, f)	X	X		
FAMILY STRUCTURE (fw, f)	X	X		
FAMILY CONTACT (fw, gt, c, f)	X	X		
INCIDENT (gt, y)		X		
BEHAVIORAL (c, y) (DAILY LIVING)	X	X		
BEHAVIORAL (t, y) (CLASSROOM)	X	X		
CLOSING (gt, y)				X

FOLLOW-UP (ra, y)	X		
EDUCATION			
INTAKE (ssw, y)			X
PSYCHOLOGICAL (ssw, y)			X
INTELLIGENCE (ssw, y)		X	X
BEHAVIORAL (t, y)		X	X
TERMINATION (t, y)	X		
SEXUAL ABUSE			
OFFENDER (d, gt, y)	X		X
VICTIM (d, gt, y)	X		X
FAMILY AT DISCLOSURE (d, fw, f)	X	X	X
FAMILY AT TERMINATION (fw, f)	X	X	X

Responsible Staff

gt group therapist
fw family worker
t teacher
c childcare worker
ra research assistant
ssw school social worker

Information Focus

d instrument completed upon disclosure of info
y information focuses on youth
f information focuses on family

41

FIGURE 1

FLOW OF INFORMATION

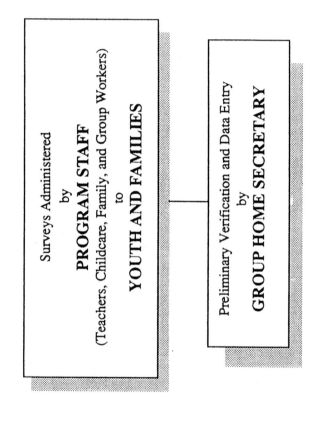

Surveys Administered
by
PROGRAM STAFF
(Teachers, Childcare, Family, and Group Workers)
to
YOUTH AND FAMILIES

Preliminary Verification and Data Entry
by
GROUP HOME SECRETARY

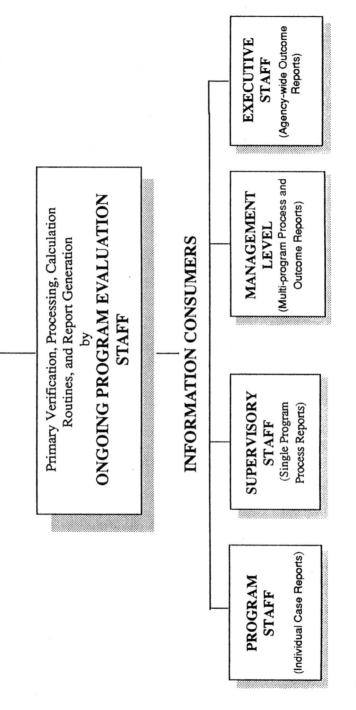

Primary Verification, Processing, Calculation Routines, and Report Generation by **ONGOING PROGRAM EVALUATION STAFF**

INFORMATION CONSUMERS

EXECUTIVE STAFF (Agency-wide Outcome Reports)

MANAGEMENT LEVEL (Multi-program Process and Outcome Reports)

SUPERVISORY STAFF (Single Program Process Reports)

PROGRAM STAFF (Individual Case Reports)

APPLICATION OF PRINCIPLES

The previous discussion has provided a general description of BOMIS that is intended to serve as a backdrop for describing management principles associated with "running" the system. The primary operating principle of the system is that line program staff are primary consumers of BOMIS information. This principle is a basis for setting departmental priorities, designing research instruments, and defining the practitioner's role in operating the system.

In an empirical study of information utilization at Boysville, Grasso, Epstein, and Tripodi (1988) suggest that utilization will only occur when the system can provide practitioners with valid and reliable information. Routine operations of BOMIS are organized around the same premise. Thus, in times of conflicting demands for information, the department's priorities are determined by proximity of an information need to the direct service practitioner.

Typical of any research department function, there are a wide variety of organizational constituencies to serve. In product terms, these constituencies demand everything from a monthly list of youths for laundry assignment to a request for a multiple regression analysis of predictors of postplacement incarceration. However, a clear set of departmental priorities exists and is applied whenever there are conflicting demands for information, the system malfunctions, or there is a need for system modifications or additions. Simply stated, whenever possible, priority is given to reporting needs of practitioners.

As a result, departmental functions receiving top priority are the verification/processing of clinical data and the generation of single case reports in a graphic format for use by agency treatment staff. If problems develop in this area, all unrelated efforts are interrupted until these difficulties can be remedied.

As indicated earlier, smooth operation in this area facilitates the receipt of valid and reliable information *from* practitioners and the feedback of timely and useful information *to* practitioners (Grasso, Epstein, & Tripodi, 1988). In addition, it is important to remember the need to have valid and reliable single case information if one is intending to aggregate information for program monitoring and evaluation.

INSTRUMENT DESIGN ISSUES

Another way in which line staff commitment to the information system and utilization is fostered is that instrument design is focused on practitioner need. Thus, research instruments that supply the data-base for BOMIS focus on the youth in placement and his/her family as the unit of analysis. This strategy allows BOMIS to provide extremely detailed treatment-relevant information to the practitioner regarding every case carried. Information needs at other levels are effectively met through aggregate reporting of practitioner information.

It is also critical for research instruments to conceptualize client/practitioner interaction in a framework that is consistent with the practitioner's treatment technology and associated frame of reference. So, for example, the family diagnostic instruments built into BOMIS are consistent with the agency's structural family therapy approach. Along the same lines, the sexual abuse instruments make use of concepts that are directly linked to the agency's training for assessment and intervention in this area.

Finally, instrument design and implementation must take into account role demands on the practitioner. Although clinicians are generally quite skillful in collecting information, this data-gathering task must always be manageable in the context of other legitimate role demands and must never appear to be an end in itself. Each Boysville practitioner has a myriad of important duties associated with treatment of individual youths and their families. It is important to view the practitioner's role in the data collection process in this light.

For example, design of the sexual abuse instrumentation deliberately centered on detailed information concerning the most recent incident of sexual abuse. This was seen as not only the most clinically relevant, but the most manageable data collection strategy for the already burdened clinician. Although the final instrument does include some questions about the client's previous experience of sexual abuse, an exhaustive and detailed history is not routinely taken. In this regard, costs in time taken from other treatment functions of collecting comprehensive and fully-detailed information concerning the client's experience with sexual abuse were judged to outweigh potential treatment benefits.

PRACTITIONER'S ROLE IN INFORMATION PROCESSING

In addition to minimizing information collection that does not have a high potential utilization benefit/cost ratio, an attempt is made to maximize "secondary" clinical benefits of information collection. For example, Boysville treatment staff are trained to administer the family assessment instrument in such a way as to promote initial engagement of the family/youth through the process of collecting clinically-relevant information.

In addition, practitioners are instructed to make qualitative observations of clients at this stage and to do an initial impressionistic review of client responses to the instruments. At this point, the completed instruments are given to a secretary for data entry and verification. The system makes no further demands on the practitioner's resources or time availabile to participate in either of these tasks.

Once verification and processing are completed by Research Department staff, the practitioner receives a graphic display of the initial assessment information. Additional verification takes place in the first instance of clinical application of this information when the treatment worker compares graphic information with his/her clinical observations and impressions.

If inconsistencies arise, the practitioner is encouraged to bring them to supervision and to challenge the data rather than automatically accept the computer output. This process promotes validity and reliability of the data-base and simultaneously increases staff assessment skills.

By involving the practitioner in information processing only when a potential clinical benefit exists, promoting the "secondary" clinical benefits of information gathering, and taking into account the multiple demands on their time, BOMIS continues to receive a relatively high level of practitioner support (Grasso, Epstein, & Tripodi, 1988).

SUMMARY

This paper has described basic elements of BOMIS and principles employed in designing, implementing, and managing the system. These principles are intended to foster treatment utilization of timely and relevant information by the agency's direct service practitioners, supervisors, administrators, and executives. The effort to enhance the effectiveness of BOMIS, expand its informational base, and foster its acceptance by agency practitioners has provided a useful framework for system development. This framework will next be applied to the development of a group work information system which will focus on group assessment and the codification of group interventions.

An underlying assumption of this paper, and a premise upon which BOMIS is designed, is that information system products should be utilized for treatment as well as for accountability purposes. Put simply, it is imperative that an effective human service information system directly address the needs of the clinical practitioners. This discussion has enumerated a variety of strategies that BOMIS staff employ for increasing its contribution to clinical decision making at Boysville. Ultimately, the practitioner's perception of the information system's usefulness will determine its success. For without practitioner legitimation, effort, and support, there is no valid or reliable information to process, analyze, or report.

REFERENCES

Blythe, B., & Briar, S. (1985). Developing empirically based models of practice. *Social Work, 30,* 483-488.

Bronson, D., Pelz, D., & Trzcinski, E. (1988). *Computerizing your agency's information system.* Newbury Park, CA: Sage Publications, Inc.

Caputo, R. (1988). *Management and information systems in human services–implications for the distribution of authority and decision making.* New York: The Haworth Press, Inc.

Conrad, K. (1985). Promoting quality of care: The role of the compliance director. *Child Welfare, 64,* 639-649.

Epstein, I., & Grasso, A. (1987). Integrating management information and program evaluation: The Boysville experience. In J. Morton, M. Balassone, & S. Guendelman (Eds.), *Preventing low birthweight and infant mortality: Programmatic issues for public health social workers.*

Epstein, I., & Grasso, A. (1990). Using agency based available information to further practice innovation. In H. Weissman (Ed.), *Serious play: Creativity and innovation in social work.* New York: NASW Press.

Grasso, A., & Epstein, I. (1987). Management by measurement: Organizational dilemmas and opportunities. *Administration in Social Work, 11,* 89-100.

Grasso, A., & Epstein, I. (1989) The Boysville Experience: Integration Practice Decision-Making, Program Evaluation, and Management Information. *Computers in Human Services, 4,* 85-95.

Grasso, A., Epstein, I., & Tripodi, T. (1988). Agency-based research utilization in a residential child care setting. *Administration in Social Work, 12,* 61-80.

Hasenfeld, Y. (1983). *Human service organizations.* Englewood Cliffs, N.J.: Prentice-Hall, Inc.

Hoshino, G. (1982). Computer tools of management and social work practice. In S. Slavin (Ed.), *Applying computers in social service and mental health agencies,* 5-10. New York: The Haworth Press, Inc.

McCarney, S. (1985). *The behavior intervention manual: Intervention strategies for behavior problems in the educational environment.* Missouri: Hawthorne Educational Services.

Olson, D., McCubbin, H., Barnes, B., Larsen, A., Muxen, M., & Wilson, M. (1982). *Family inventories.* University of Minnesota: Department of Family Social Science.

Mutschler, E., & Hasenfeld, Y. (1986). Integrated information systems for social work practice. *Social Work, 31,* 345-349.

Reid, W. J. (1980). Research strategies for improving individualized services. In D. Fanshel (Ed.), *Future of social work research.* Washington, D.C.: National Association of Social Workers, 38-52.

Walker, R. (1972). The ninth panacea: Program evaluation. *Evaluation, 1,* 45-53.

Wechsler, D., (1974). *Manual for the intelligence scale for children-revised.* New York: Psychological Corporation.

Woodcock, R. W., & Johnson, M. B. (1977). *Woodcock-Johnson psycho-educational battery.* Texas: DLM Teaching Resources.

The Use
of an Agency-Based Information System
in Structural Family Therapy Treatment

John Mooradian
Anthony J. Grasso

ABSTRACT. Social workers have always relied on information about clients and their environment in making practice decisions. When this information is systematized and conceptualized as "research," however, workers tend to respond negatively to programmatic efforts to incorporate it into their practice. This paper describes the critical role of Boysville's Office of Clinical Staff Development in training family workers to employ BOMIS information in their clinical practice.

Whether recognizing it or not, social workers have always been committed to an "information-driven" approach to service delivery (Tratner, 1979). Thus, irrespective of the model of practice employed and the presence or absence of computers, social workers have always relied on in-

---

John Mooradian is affiliated with Boysville of Michigan, 8744 Clinton-Macon Road, Clinton, MI 49236. Anthony J. Grasso is Director, School of Social Work, University of Nevada at Las Vegas, 4505 Maryland Parkway, Las Vegas, NV 89154-5032.

[Haworth co-indexing entry note]: "The Use of an Agency-Based Information System in Structural Family Therapy Treatment." Mooradian, John, and Anthony J. Grasso. Co-published simultaneously in *Child & Youth Services*, (The Haworth Press, Inc.) Vol. 16, No. 1, 1993, pp. 49-74; and: *Information Systems in Child, Youth, and Family Agencies: Planning, Implementation, and Service Enhancement* (ed: Anthony J. Grasso, and Irwin Epstein) The Haworth Press, Inc., 1993, pp. 49-74. Multiple copies of this article/chapter may be purchased from The Haworth Document Delivery Center. Call 1-800-3-HAWORTH (1-800-342-9678) between 9:00 - 5:00 (EST) and ask for DOCUMENT DELIVERY CENTER.

49

formation about the client and his or her environment for making practice decisions. Attempts to systematize their use of information, however, especially when referred to invidiously as "research," have generally met with indifference, fear, defensiveness, and hostility.

The objections many clinicians raise concerning efforts to systematize the use of information in practice decision making is that these approaches are mechanistic, deny the significance of clinical intuition, thwart spontaneity, and rely too much on quantitative data. In this context, quantitative measures are viewed as antithetical to qualitative and incompatible with the humanistic character of clinical practice (Epstein, 1985). This mistaken belief has severely limited the range of alternatives available to practitioners for assessment, intervention planning, monitoring and evaluation (Tripodi & Epstein, 1980). An unfortunate and paradoxical consequence of the rejection of research-based techniques and procedures in the name of humanistic practice is that the result may be less effective service delivery to clients.

In order to successfully integrate BOMIS information into clinical decision making at Boysville, a departmental Office of Clinical Staff Development (OCSD) was created with the primary responsibility of translating computerized information into direct service practice interventions. Rothman (1974) describes this organizational function as the provision of specialists in linking research information to direct practice utilization. OCSD is completely dedicated to this function because it is central to the clinical integration of BOMIS information.

From the start, BOMIS planners recognized that the greater the demands placed on clinical workers to independently translate BOMIS information into direct practice decisions, the less likely the information would be used. In addition, it was felt this translation function required specific skills not yet possessed by today's social work practitioners (Lippitt, 1966; Havelock, 1969; Rothman, 1974). Further, computer-generated information assumes linear patterns of causality which creates additional problems since social work practice seems to rest more on interactive, multi-causal models.

As a result, we know that giving computerized information directly to practitioners without specific training in ongoing use would reduce the likelihood that they would draw correct conclusions from reports, no matter what the report format. Finally, like the direct service practitioner, we also feared that without having the experiential process of teaching staff how to use BOMIS information within the context of more traditional case supervision, important qualitative information and interpretation not incorporated into BOMIS might be disregarded under the weight of an automated process.

After considering these issues, Boysville's administration decided to commit 16 positions to OCSD in order to fully support this translation and education function. In a later section of this article which deals with the use of BOMIS in family therapy, more detail is given to the actual process of training staff to use BOMIS information, and case examples are provided. The next section, however, gives greater detail about the rationale for creating OCSD, its organization, and the training structures it routinely employs.

THE OFFICE OF CLINICAL STAFF DEVELOPMENT

Since the inception of BOMIS, Boysville has found many prospective treatment staff, even those with recent graduate educations, were inadequately prepared to meet service needs of its clients. Job applicants had generally received no training in the use of quantitative information designed to aid practice decision making. The need at Boysville for simultaneous expertise in treatment, teamwork, research and information utilization, and outreach to families required intensive, coordinated educational efforts on the part of the agency and the learning of many specific skills by new workers.

More generally, in accordance with Boysville's conception of itself as a learning/teaching agency, professional skills development for all Boysville staff is seen as a continuing process. This conception is not unique to Boysville. What is unique, however, is the effort to directly link the provision of quality service to clients, making full and appropriate use of BOMIS-generated information.

As a result, with the advent of BOMIS, the agency expanded and formalized its previous training programs, charging OCSD with the responsibility of providing education/training for all treatment staff and the development of extensive training models to be used by other agencies. Training is conceptually integrated and applied across Boysville's diverse programs and sites. It is individually designed for each staff member so that veteran staff are updated, mid-level staff proceed steadily toward greater competency, and entry-level staff have a sufficient base for competent, beginning work.

The Director of OCSD is an MSW with a concentration in interpersonal practice and extensive experience in clinical practice and training. Fifteen clinical supervisors report directly to the director and have specific areas of practice specialty for which they are responsible. These areas of specialty are: Family Treatment, Group Work, Group Living, Education, Foster Care and Home-Based Services. The first four specialties are grouped into three teams with a Family Treatment, Group Work, and Group Living and Educational Clinical supervisor on each team. These teams have responsibility for training in different Boysville regional areas. The remaining three OCSD professional staff are responsible for training in the Foster Care, In-Home Care, and Home Builders programs.

Training takes place within two distinct formats–classroom presentations given once weekly by specialty and weekly team supervision/training sessions. Clinical materials used and topics discussed are, whenever possible, related to current cases carried by treatment staff. In this way, practitioners are given direct experiential referents in all training. General practice principles taught are applied to these cases as well.

THE USE OF BOMIS IN FAMILY THERAPY

Through staff training, OCSD attempts to bridge the perceived and actual gap between quantitative, clinically-oriented BOMIS information and clinical practice. This takes place within the context of a family therapy treatment modality which routinely employs both quantitative and qualitative data in the assessment, monitoring and evaluation of individuals and families in treatment.

In order to structure a training program that would achieve this end, it was initially necessary for clinical staff to specify choice of treatment modality and for Boysville's Research Department to locate and/or design diagnostic assessment, treatment monitoring, and treatment evaluation instruments which provided information compatible with the preferred treatment modality. It was also necessary to design and implement organizational support structures to train, supervise, and reinforce practitioners for proper use of the quantitative information provided by the information system.

However well designed and implemented, the understanding, integration, and application of a clinical information system was, and continues to be, a developmental challenge for all staff. The process of meeting this challenge can be divided into four stages of staff response: awareness, anxiety, acceptance, and application. Careful planning, training, and clinical supervision were necessary to facilitate this developmental process. At the beginning of this process, Boysville treatment staff with varying degrees of clinical and research competency and different treatment orientations, had to be taught to question their own and each other's practice perceptions, implicit practice theories and hypotheses, and routine interventions. These stages of staff response to OCSD training efforts will be elaborated later in this article. Next is described the evolution of Boysville's approach to clinical treatment as a total agency.

HISTORY OF TREATMENT MODALITIES
EMPLOYED AT BOYSVILLE

At this point in its history, Boysville provides both short- and long-term treatment for adolescents and their families. Youths in care are referred by courts as either adjudicated delinquents or dependent/neglected wards. These youths have exhibited serious acting-out behaviors and demonstrated poor judgment in home, school, and community. Their offenses range from home and school truancy to serious felony offenses including criminal sexual conduct and homicide.

Although Boysville currently provides individually-oriented pastoral counseling, group work, and family treatment, it has not always done so. In fact, in recent years, the agency has fundamentally re-shaped the conception of its "client" from an individual youth in placement to a youth *and* his family. Correlative with this change in perspective has been an expansion in the range of treatment technologies offered by the agency. As a result, family therapy and more sophisticated group intervention methods have been routinely incorporated into service delivery.

Boysville's group work approach to work with delinquents began in the early 1970s. Its early group treatment model was Positive Peer Culture (Vorrath & Brendtro, 1974). Ultimately, this was combined with elements from Reality Therapy (Glasser, 1965) and Interpersonal Group Therapy (Yalom, 1985).

Despite the recognized value of these group intervention methods, early evaluation efforts convinced staff that treating youth in isolation from their families and communities was less effective than desired. This awareness led to further evolution in the Boysville treatment approach. In 1981, the decision was made to incorporate some type of family treatment into the work with every youth in placement.

Notwithstanding this general commitment to working with the family, no particular model of family therapy was adopted or consistently applied until 1983. In that year, Br. James Caley, Boysville's first OCSD Director, committed himself and the agency to the practice of Structural Family Therapy (Minuchin & Fishman, 1981). This decision was based on the fact that many of the operative concepts in Structural Family Therapy had conceptual and theoretical parallels in Boysville's existing group treatment paradigm. In addition, the emphasis this form of family treatment placed upon empowerment of the family through development of internal strength was philosophically congruent with the agency's current mission and future direction. The former involves a commitment to client empowerment, the latter to seeking alternatives to institutional placement. As a result, Structural Family Therapy was officially adopted as Boysville's framework for family assessment and intervention.

Once officially adopted, the process of integrating this form of family therapy into the existing treatment program remained complex and fraught with both attitudinal and logistical difficulties. Despite theoretical compatibility, the effort to routinely incorporate this new treatment technology into the pre-agency's existing service delivery system met with resistance. Some clinical and administrative staff members attempted to isolate family therapy practitioners.

The organizational and ideological opponents of structural family therapy continued to view working with families as inherently in conflict with the group treatment model then employed at Boysville. At best, they considered family therapy an unnecessary and frivolous addition to the agency's treatment program. At times, open conflict was expressed between groups of staff committed to one or the other treatment approach.

In this regard, Boysville's experience is not unique. Thus, it is quite similar to the process described by others who have attempted to integrate family treatment into their agency's treatment technology (McConkey-Radetzki, 1987). What distinguishes Boysville from other settings, however, is the manner in which the subsequent introduction of an agency-based information system served as a structural device to facilitate the integration process.

TREATMENT INSTRUMENTS AND REPORTS

The information system designed for use by treatment workers at Boysville involves the collection of data relevant at both the individual and family system levels and the routine generation of reports intended to enhance practice decision making. Specific instruments developed at the University of Minnesota were chosen for inclusion in BOMIS because they were based upon key Structural Family Therapy concepts and theory (Olson, McCubbin et al., 1982) and addressed individual and family variables.

For example, instruments focusing on the individual include the A-FILE and the A-COPES. The A-FILE (i.e., Adolescent-Family Inventory of Life Events and Changes) examines life changes and stressful events which the adolescent may have experienced during the course of his/her development. This instrument identifies the occurrence of major life events and changes within the context of family life. The A-FILE divides occurrence of family life events and changes into six general categories (transitions, sexuality, losses, responsibilities and strains, substance use, and legal conflict), distinguishing between a normative and non-normative range in frequency of events.

For analytic purposes, these events are also divided temporally into the immediately preceding twelve-month period and the adolescent's life prior to that twelve-month period. Based upon these data, BOMIS routinely generates a graphic printout which describes the youth's developmental experience for the practitioners' use (Figure 1).

The A-COPES (Adolescent Coping Orientation for Problem Experiences) was designed to identify those behaviors that adolescents find most helpful in managing problems or difficult situations. Using data from this instrument, a graphic printout is routinely produced by BOMIS for each youth in placement which describes the youth's coping skills along twelve scaler dimensions (Ventilation, Low Level Activity, Self Reliance and Positive Response, Emotional Connections, Family Problem Solving, Passive Problem Solving, Spiritual Support, Close Friendship Support, Professional Support, High Activity Level, Humor, and Relaxation) (Figure 2).

Instruments focused on the family include the F-COPES and the FACES II. The F-COPES (Family Crisis Oriented Personal Evaluation Scales) was developed to identify problem-solving and stress reduction behavior strategies employed by the family. This information comes from adult family members in response to specific problems or difficulties. Based upon their responses, BOMIS routinely provides numerical printouts to staff which display family responses in relation to five scaler dimensions (Social Support, Reframing, Spiritual Support, Mobilization of Resources, and Passive Appraisal), together with an overall score (Figure 3).

FACES II (Family Adaptability and Cohesion Evaluation Scale) was developed to measure family problem-solving abilities and how family members relate with one another. The instrument measures these aspects along two primary dimensions–adaptability and cohesion. Adaptability relates to the ability of a family sub-system to change its power structure, role relationships, and relationship rules in response to situational and developmental stress. Sub-dimensions of adaptability are assertiveness, leadership, discipline, negotiation, roles, and rules. Cohesion is the emotional closeness within family relationships. Sub-dimensions of cohesion are emotional bonding, external boundaries, coalitions, time, space, friendship, decision making, and interests and recreation.

On the FACES II instrument, all family members are asked to indicate

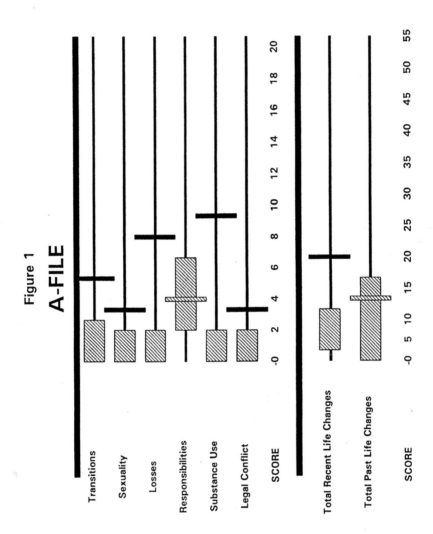

Figure 1
A-FILE

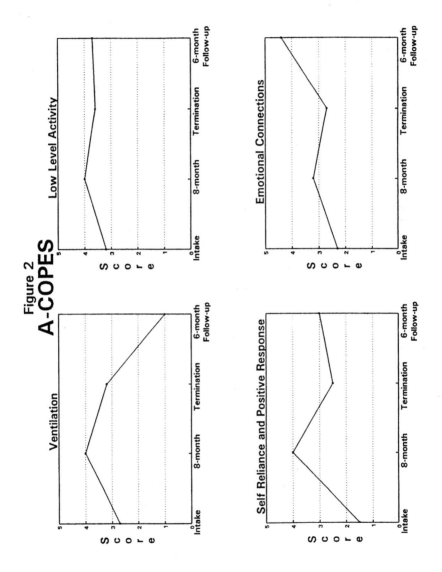

Figure 2
A-COPES

Figure 2 (continued)
A-COPES

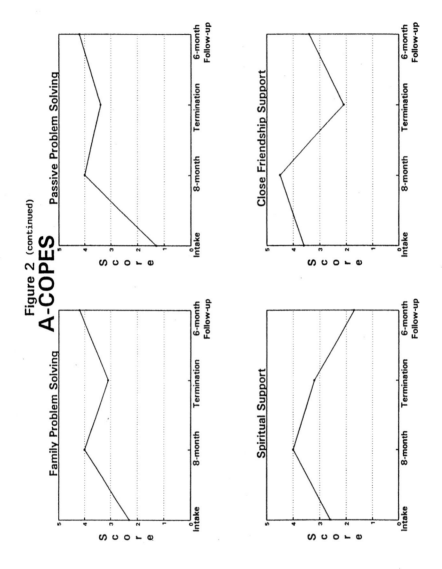

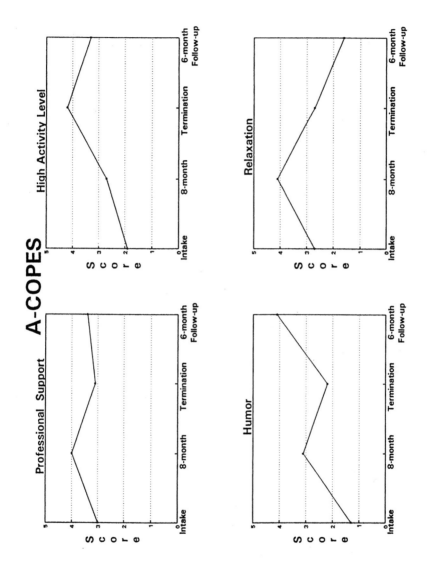

A-COPES

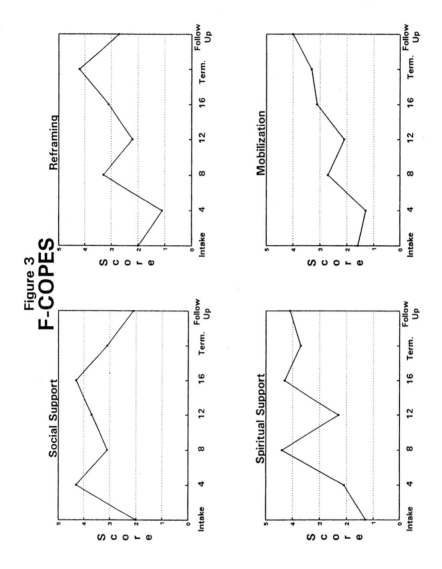

Figure 3
F-COPES

F-COPES

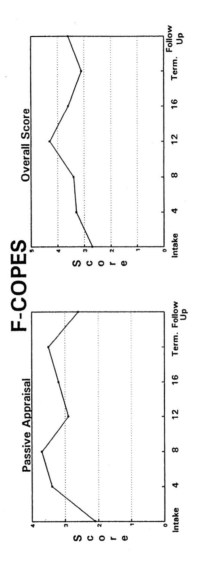

their perception related to each item in the current state (the "Real" response) and how they would like things to be (the "Ideal" response). This dual response format allows for comparison of "Real" and "Ideal" perceptions for youths in placement as well as for other family members. Discrepancies between "Real" and "Ideal" are used by treatment staff to indicate the sources and extent of dissatisfaction with family functioning for each family member (Figure 4).

Based upon FACES II data, in addition to the routinely produced graphic printouts, a grid is used to help the worker locate the family on the Circumplex Model of family functioning, including both its "Real" and "Ideal" status in terms of the model's subcategories of adaptability (chaotic, flexible, structured, rigid) and cohesion (disengaged, separated, connected, enmeshed) (Figure 5).

A numerical printout is also produced which displays all family members' responses for the "Real" and "Ideal" components of each sub-dimension. By displaying all family members' responses on one report, systemic family characteristics and problems can be more easily identified by family treatment workers. These include conflicting alignments of family members on the various sub-dimensions.

A final instrument, the Family Contact Report, is used as a measure of staff activity. This instrument is completed by staff members who make contact with any family member of the youth in placement. Although the instrument can be used to monitor Family Worker activity in the treatment team, it was primarily designed to produce a measure of worker process useful in individual staff professional development as well as in overall program planning. This instrument also provides some limited information on differing intervention approaches such as face-to-face versus telephone contacts with family members.

From the family contact instrument, a numerical report is regularly generated which provides information on who was involved in the contact, location of the contact, type of meeting, theme of the session, category of therapeutic intervention used, evaluative assessment of the interaction itself, and the length of the meeting in minutes. This report is provided to the Clinical Supervisor who periodically reviews information with individual workers.

As described earlier, to facilitate the use of reports and the information they contain by direct service practitioners, OCSD employs a sizable, full-time training/clinical supervision staff. These individuals are all experienced clinicians who have received special training for their roles as "translators" of research information into practice application. OCSD trainers and clinical supervisors operate on the principle that effective staff

Figure 4
FACES-II

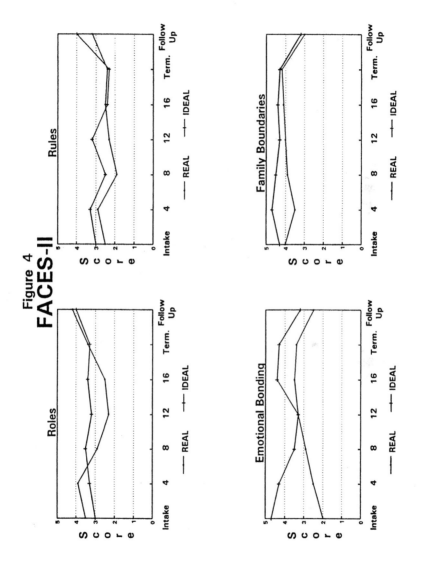

63

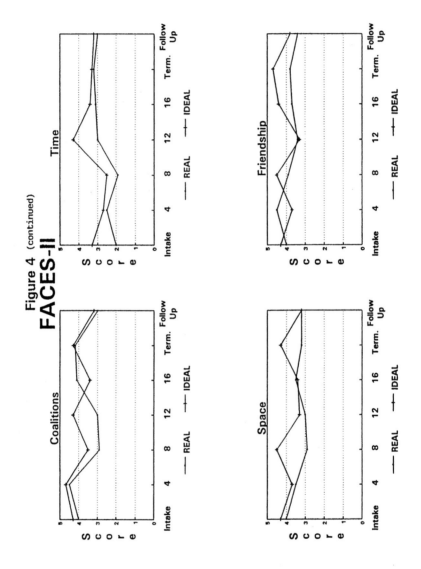

Figure 4 (continued)
FACES-II

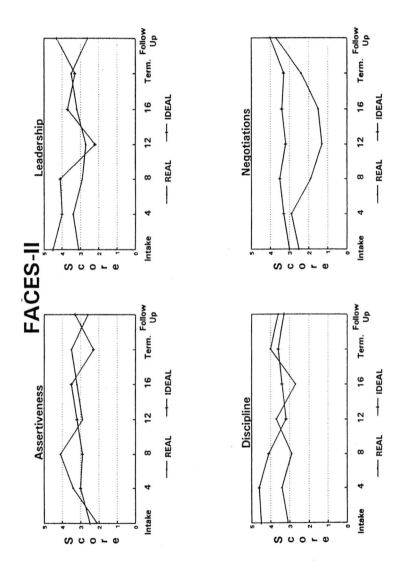

FACES-II

Assertiveness

— REAL   —†— IDEAL

Leadership

— REAL   —†— IDEAL

Discipline

— REAL   —†— IDEAL

Negotiations

— REAL   —†— IDEAL

Figure 4 (continued)
FACES-II

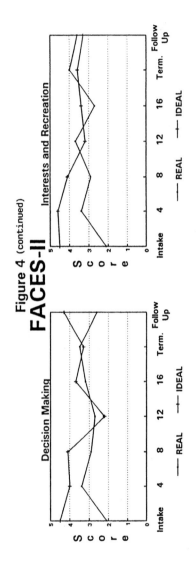

Figure 5

FACES-II
Circumplex Model

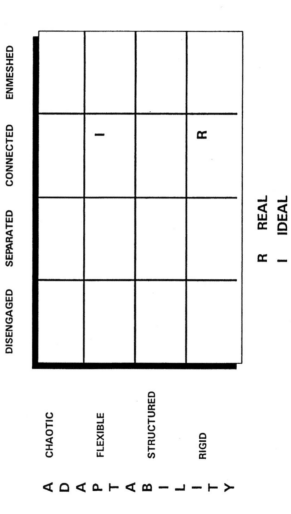

C O H E S I O N

DISENGAGED   SEPARATED   CONNECTED   ENMESHED

A CHAOTIC
D
A
P FLEXIBLE
T
A
B STRUCTURED
I
L
I RIGID
T
Y

I

R

R   REAL
I   IDEAL

67

development leads to improved service delivery. Their overall strategy is to increase practitioner use of BOMIS information by decreasing practitioner effort required to process and interpret it and by demonstrating its successful practice applications.

To further develop practitioners' skills at BOMIS report reading, interpretation, and application, OCSD staff engage in a full range of educational and supervisory activities. These include general training sessions, individual case reviews, videotape reviews, and live supervision. Irrespective of the medium used, movement toward practice utilization of the information system for clinical decision making has proven to be a complex developmental process. The following sections provide a description of the stages of staff response to this process.

AWARENESS

In the first attempt at clinical implementation of the information system, OCSD training staff focused on informing family treatment workers about the range of individual and family information made available through BOMIS and the treatment relevance of this information. Basic treatment concepts which were tapped by the data-collection instruments were systematically illustrated. Potential practice applications of each of these dimensions and sub-dimensions were considered as well.

One of the more successful training devices used to promote treatment staff awareness of the clinical potential of the new information system involved doing "autopsies" of treatment failures based on a FACES II analysis of what might have gone wrong. So, for example, at one Family Worker General Training Session, a practitioner presented a case in which a Boysville youth from a single-parent family was arrested for assault and battery three months post-release.

FACES II, along with the other instruments, had been administered to the youth and his family during an early period in the development of the information system. At that time, however, there was as yet no training offered to staff regarding the application of this information to decision making with clients. Hence, although the information was available, it was not used by the practitioner in family assessment or in the provision of treatment to this family.

In this particular case, through the course of treatment, the youth in placement had demonstrated increased responsibility and interpersonal skills in his residential treatment group. At the same time, the mother of the youth had made a substantial effort to become more involved in the community and to increase her own leadership, disciplinary, and decision-making skills. Moreover, she had recently enrolled in college. As a result, she was clearly more empowered in her family and her community. Because of the positive changes in behavior of both the youth and his mother, the treatment worker recommended that the youth be returned to his family.

FACES II data introduced into the case review, however, revealed heretofore unrecognized problems. On the final FACES II instruments completed by the youth and by his mother prior to discharge, there was a sizable discrepancy between the youth's "Real" and "Ideal" scores on the family sub-dimensions of leadership, discipline, and decision making. This discrepancy indicated considerable dissatisfaction on the youth's part with his role in the family. There was no such discrepancy for the mother. In other words, the FACES II data revealed that although the youth shared his mother's perceptions of her "Real" recent changes, he did not agree that these changes were "Ideal." In fact, he experienced them as quite undesirable.

Unfortunately, although the youth's participation in the group treatment program and the mother's involvement in the family treatment program appeared to successfully address the respective functioning and behavior of each, the discrepancies between their "Real" and "Ideal" conceptions of treatment outcomes went unaddressed. Consequently, even though the youth participated actively in group and family treatment sessions, the two treatment approaches were not successfully integrated. Apparently the youth, full of high expectations based on recent in-program success, wanted to take a more active role in leading his family. Although his mother had abdicated her parental responsibility to him in the past, she now felt more confident and capable of taking on her proper parental leadership role. Consequently, she now resisted his attempts to resume the role as family leader. In the language of Structural Family Therapy, she no longer needed or wanted a diffuse parent/child sub-system boundary. He did.

The desire on his part to regain the role of family leader was further evidenced in an offense for which he was subsequently arrested. Hence, after frustrated attempts to regain his authority within the family, the youth assaulted a neighbor who threatened his brother. In this context, this act could now be interpreted as the youth's effort to reclaim and demonstrate the protective role of a parent.

Had the FACES II information regarding the discrepancy between "Real" and "Ideal" conceptions of individual and family functioning been available and comprehensible to the family therapist involved in the case, more effort could have been directed toward supporting an appropriate sense of responsibility for the youth in his reconstructed family, the reorganization of which involved more clearly defined adult/child boundaries.

Clearly, the process of case review using dramatic examples such as this, offered compelling evidence to staff of the utility of the information that was newly available through BOMIS. The impact of this case review on some of the agency's practitioners was sufficient to motivate them to seek to develop skills in applying computerized information to other cases. Nevertheless, it remained apparent during this stage of development of the information and training systems that more had to be done to increase the practitioners' awareness of the usefulness of the information to their direct practice decision making.

In general, then, an information systems approach which linked conceptual categories and theoretical frameworks with Boysville's treatment technology was used to increase awareness on the part of practitioners of BOMIS' clinical utility. Additional training efforts emphasized the use of instruments in assessing, monitoring, and evaluating clinical work with individuals and their families.

Full days of training were set aside for agency practitioners to focus on the A-FILE, A-COPES, F-COPES, and FACES II and their uses in conjunction with conventional "process" record material and clinical observation. This extensive effort served to bring about an increased awareness of the utility of the instruments and a decreased adherence to the view that quantitative, computerized data and clinically-relevant information are inherently incompatible.

ANXIETY

Despite increasing staff awareness of the potential for information use, they still used denial and avoidance to resist change during early stages of implementation of the information system. At that time, it became clear that awareness of the utility of the instruments was not sufficient to motivate all clinicians to actually use the information. Many acknowledged its availability but denied its utility.

So, for example, in an empirical study of changes in staff attitudes towards the information system, 52% of Boysville's professional staff remained skeptical about the utility of BOMIS a year after its introduction (Grasso, Epstein, & Tripodi, 1988).

Resistant staff who avoided administering the research instruments or using the information in their practice justified their non-utilization with the following explanations: (1) a lack of confidence in the validity, reliability and accuracy of the data received; (2) a lack of understanding of the instruments and reports; and (3) a lack of opportunity to apply the information to their clinical practice. Moreover, despite continued assertions and assurances by Clinical Supervisors that the information system was designed to improve service effectiveness and practitioners' skills, many remained suspicious that the primary purpose of the system was to observe individual worker performance and to punish those who were not in compliance with performance standards.

During this stage of implementation, the intended pattern of administration of the data-gathering instruments on a four-month cycle could not be achieved. Workers reported a distressingly large number of families "refusing" to complete the instruments. Or they contended that families could not be located when scheduled testing was to take place.

Upon further investigation, it became apparent that although OCSD staff were emphasizing the clinical utility of BOMIS, some Program Managers were subverting clinical application of the information system by instructing direct service workers that they need only comply with the requirement to administer the instruments. In other words, the message was "get the forms filled out on time, but practice as you had done before." Even the administration of instruments was characterized by some as a useless and time-consuming chore to satisfy the "academic" research purposes of Boysville's consultants.

Naturally, this pattern of managerial subversion resulted in a continued resistance by treatment staff to gathering and utilizing the BOMIS information for service delivery purposes. Once this came to light, a few managers continued their effort to block information utilization despite explicit warnings against it. Ultimately the negative effects of these managers were neutralized through the continued use of the case review approach referred to in the foregoing section. Mooradian and Grasso (in preparation) describe this process in greater detail elsewhere. Suffice it to say, this training approach finally achieved a fair degree of attitudinal integration on the part of clinical staff.

ACCEPTANCE

Although individual agency practitioners varied greatly in their degree of acceptance of the information's utility in the avoidance stage, over time, they gradually came to accept and legitimate the information system. In this "acceptance stage," staff demonstrated a more complete conceptual understanding of the dimensions and sub-dimensions measured by instruments and their intended clinical utility. Through further training and continued clinical supervision, more sophisticated diagnostic and treatment applications were demonstrated and further attitudinal commitment to BOMIS utilization was secured.

As is the case with all skills-training programs, however, participants cannot learn to apply the skills they are taught without being given structured opportunities to do so. At Boysville, specific opportunities needed to be provided for clinicians to apply new concepts and techniques they had learned directly to cases with which they were currently engaged. Clinical supervisory activity during this stage of BOMIS' development was focused on teaching practitioners new bases for conceptualizing their clients' problems and related treatment approaches. Case reviews, joint supervision of group workers and family therapists, and live supervision of family therapy sessions as well as videotape reviews, were all based on information from the instruments, used in conjunction with current qualitative case information.

Predictably, practitioners who most quickly accepted these organizational changes were those who had a prior commitment to the theory and practice of Structural Family Therapy, and/or those who were newest to the agency. Obviously, the former saw the information as congruent with their own therapeutic ideology and as providing a tool for improved service delivery. The newcomers, on the other hand, recognized that this approach represented the future orientation of the agency and were relatively quick to sign on. Indeed, some were attracted to the agency because of the emphasis on practice-research utilization.

Since Clinical Supervisors remained steadfast in their insistence that information based upon the administration of the instruments was an integral part of their supervision, some supervisory sessions with highly resistive staff members were at times conflictual. In fact, some were canceled when practitioners did not bring relevant BOMIS reports to supervisory meetings. Although this occurred in relatively few instances, word of it got around, and managers were urged by agency administration to support the Clinical Supervisors' position. This structurally reinforced the message that the information was a central component of clinical practice and service delivery at the agency. Not surprisingly, where Program Managers were most supportive of Clinical Supervisors, treatment worker acceptance was highest.

APPLICATION

It has been noted by many clinical writers that the fundamental goal of clinical supervision is to develop practitioners' skills to the point where they actually surpass their supervisors in the application of these skills (Minuchin & Fishman, 1981; Breunlin, Liddle, & Schwartz, 1988). This principle guided supervisors in the process of teaching practitioners to use BOMIS information. Since these informational tools had never been available to the supervisors before, they needed to be comfortable with the fact that their supervisees, once successfully trained, might accomplish more with their clients and families than the supervisors had in the past.

With this possibility in mind, Clinical Supervisors were encouraged to teach practitioners how to learn more about client systems through use of systematically gathered, quantitative information. And, whereas the focus during the acceptance stage was on making the instruments an integral part of the supervision process, emphasis during the application phase was on making the information generated by practitioners an integral part of diagnostic assessment and treatment planning, service delivery, and treatment evaluation.

The focus of the training effort at this point in the process was on increasing the creative range and type of worker application of BOMIS information to practice. In addition, they were encouraged to generalize and test their insights with other treatment cases. At the time of this writing, there are still sizable differences in clinical staff commitment to utilization of information in practice decision making (Grasso, Epstein, & Tripodi, 1988). Nevertheless, the organizational culture and structure surrounding and supporting the information system has improved remarkably. With that change, basic attitudes and practices of the clinical staff have also shifted. Today, practitioners who make statements about how numbers and clinical practice are incompatible are likely to be discredited by their peers. In fact, some clinicians themselves have become the "disciples" of this new information approach to helping clients. Happily, the pockets of staff resistance to this effort are disappearing. Hopefully, the application stage signals the institutionalization of BOMIS utilization in agency practice.

More generally, in its approach to family treatment training and supervision, the Boysville experience has shown that under proper organizational conditions, clinicians can increase their own effectiveness through application of an integrated agency-based information system. To accomplish this, such an information system must be congruent with practitioners' conceptual and theoretical frameworks as well as their established treatment paradigms. Ultimately, such an approach must demonstrably improve the quality, effectiveness, and efficiency of practice. At the very least, such a system has the potential to refute its own claims to superiority. This cannot be said for many other therapeutic approaches.

Even under the best of conditions, however, the evolution of such a system requires that staff go through a predictable set of stages that include awareness, anxiety, acceptance, and application. Formal supervisory and administrative practices as well as informal processes can facilitate or impede this process. The successful integration of information systems with service delivery requires all of the above.

REFERENCES

Breunlin, D. C., Liddle, H. A., & Schwartz R. C. (1988). Concurrent training of supervisors and therapists. In H. A. Liddle, D. C. Breunlin, & R. C. Schwartz (Eds.), *Handbook of family therapy training and supervision*. New York: The Guilford Press.

Epstein, I. (1985). Quantitative and qualitative research methods: Conflict or continuum. In R. Grinnell, Jr. (Ed.), *Research in social work*. 2nd edition. Itasca, IL: Peacock Press.

Glasser, W. (1965). *Reality therapy*. New York: Harper and Row.

Grasso A., Epstein I., & Tripodi T. (1988). Agency-based research utilization in a residential child care setting. *Administration in Social Work, 12*, 61-80.

Havelock, R. G. (1969). *Planning for innovations: Through dissemination and utilization of knowledge*. Ann Arbor, Michigan: Institute for Social Research.

Lippitt, R. (1966). The process of utilization of social research to improve social practice. In A. B. Shostak (Ed.), *Sociology in action: Case studies in social problems and directed social change*. Homewood, IL: The Dorsey Press.

McConkey-Radetzki, N. (1987). Development of a family therapy program in a residential treatment setting. *Journal of Systemic and Strategic Therapies,.6.*

Minuchin, S., & Fishman, C. (1981). *Family therapy techniques*. Cambridge, MA: Harvard University Press.

Mooradian, J., & Grasso, A. (In preparation). The use of an agency-based information system in structural family therapy training.

Olson, D., McCubbin, H., Barnes, B., Larsen, A., Muxen, M., & Wilson, M. (1982). *Family inventories*. University of Minnesota: Family Social Science.

Rothman, J. (1974). *Planning and organizing for social change*. New York: Columbia University Press.

Tratner, W. (1979). *From poor law to welfare state*. 2nd Edition. New York: Free Press, Macmillan Publishing Company.

Tripodi, T., & Epstein, I. (1980). *Research techniques for clinical social work*. New York: Columbia University Press.

Vorrath, H. H., & Brendtro, L. (1974). *Positive peer culture*. Chicago, IL: Aldine.

Yalom, I. D. (1985). *The theory and practice of group pychotherapy*. New York: Basic Books.

SECTION TWO

Principles
for Using Management Information Data
for Programmatic Decision Making

Br. Chester Freel
Irwin Epstein

ABSTRACT. This paper describes administrative practice principles for the effective use of management information systems data in making program-level decisions. It is based on the assumption that a properly constructed information system can serve both external accountability requirements and internal administrative needs. This dual use of management information enhances the quality, effectiveness, and efficiency of the program. Illustrations of this are drawn from the Boysville experience.

Since the 1970s, residential child care agencies have been increasingly required to demonstrate achievement of prescribed performance goals (Young, 1978). This increased pressure for accountability has come primarily from external sources such as funding and regulatory agencies. As

---

Br. Chester Freel is affiliated with Boysville of Michigan, 8744 Clinton-Macon Road, Clinton, MI 49236. Irwin Epstein is affiliated with the School of Social Work, Hunter College, City University of New York, 129 East 79th Street, New York, NY 10021.

[Haworth co-indexing entry note]: "Principles for Using Management Information Data for Programmatic Decision Making." Freel, Br. Chester, and Irwin Epstein. Co-published simultaneously in *Child & Youth Services,* (The Haworth Press, Inc.) Vol. 16, No. 1, 1993, pp. 77-93; and: *Information Systems in Child, Youth, and Family Agencies: Planning, Implementation, and Service Enhancement* (ed: Anthony J. Grasso, and Irwin Epstein) The Haworth Press, Inc., 1993, pp. 77-93. Multiple copies of this article/chapter may be purchased from The Haworth Document Delivery Center. Call 1-800-3-HAWORTH (1-800-342-9678) between 9:00 - 5:00 (EST) and ask for DOCUMENT DELIVERY CENTER.

a result, many agencies like Boysville have developed management information and reporting systems for describing and evaluating programs for youths and their families (Grasso & Epstein, 1989; Weber & Polansky, 1975).

While the dominant concern of the 70s might have been accountability, the concern of the 80s has been survival (Bielawski & Epstein, 1984). These two themes are linked, however, since agency and program survival depend in part on the ability to document quantity and quality of service delivery. This pressure for documentation is expected to continue into the 90s (Austin et al., 1982).

Despite the increasing use of information systems for external accountability, many program managers fail to recognize that the same data bases constructed for *external* accountability purposes can be used to maintain and improve *internal* service delivery (Austin et al., 1982; Young, 1978; Hoshino, 1978).

There are several reasons why program managers often fail to recognize the potential usefulness of information systems for programmatic decision making. First, external evaluators routinely ask different questions than do program managers. While the former are likely to ask whether a program is worth initiating or sustaining, the latter are more likely to ask how an existing program can be improved. Despite these differences in vantage point, however, if the right kinds of program data are collected and packaged correctly, both kinds of questions can be answered (Grasso, Epstein, & Tripodi, 1988).

Second, program managers in social work agencies are likely to be social workers trained as clinicians (Patti & Austin, 1977). As a result, they are generally unfamiliar with the application of information systems to day-to-day, programmatic decision making (Weber & Polansky, 1975). Even when managers appreciate the value of program evaluation, they often find research concepts, instruments, and techniques confusing and intimidating.

What information is relevant for what decisions? How do we arrive at appropriate performance indicators? How much data must we collect before it has meaning? Can one conduct meaningful research without control groups? What do we do if results of the evaluation indicate we are doing a poor job? All these questions and many more confront the social work manager who entertains the programmatic use of information systems data. Mistakenly, managers often assume that only researchers and "academic types" can answer these questions. However with proper training and involvement in the development and ongoing implementation of the information system, managers can be effective consumers and utilizers of evaluation data (Grasso & Epstein, 1987).

A third reason for the failure of managers to employ these kinds of data is the mistaken belief that evaluation research takes place only after a program has been completed. Contrary to this belief, when properly packaged and fed back, management information and program evaluation data can be employed for programmatic decision making throughout the development of a program (Tripodi, Fellin, & Epstein, 1978).

This process may be compared to a cook making soup. The cook periodically runs a spoon through the soup while it is cooking to secure a sample of the broth, to taste it, and add this or that ingredient to bring the soup up to his or her standards of taste. In much the same way, the program manager can employ information systems data for making inferences about program performance based on specific programmatic criteria and for making necessary programmatic adjustments to improve service delivery (Hoshino, 1978).

A fourth reason that managers do not take programmatic advantage of information systems data is that, like most social workers in most childcare agencies, program managers are likely to have heavy workloads and excessive demands placed on their time. Because of this, working with MIS and program evaluation data may seem like a luxury item that managers can little afford. Contrary to this belief, however, the proper use of information systems data can contribute to managerial as well as program efficiency and program effectiveness.

Finally, clinically-trained program managers often fear that employing quantitative data necessitates the dehumanization of clients and staff and the abandonment of clinical judgment. On the contrary, the proper use of management information and program evaluation data involves an interaction between research information, clinical judgment, and program observation. This enriches rather than diminishes our understanding of clients, workers, and the programs in which they interact with each other.

The purpose of this paper is to describe practice principles for the effective use of management information data in making programmatic decisions. To illustrate the application of these principles, examples are drawn from the Boysville experience. The paper begins with the assumption that a properly constructed data base can serve both external accountability and internal decision making functions. Moreover, it assumes that the dual use of management information data enhances the quality, effectiveness, and efficiency of the services we provide.

MANAGEMENT COMMITMENT
TO INFORMATION-DRIVEN DECISION MAKING

Management information systems (MIS) can serve the dual functions of external accountability and internal programmatic decision making only when they are constructed with both in mind. To ensure this wherever possible, managers should be involved early in the development of an information system and in decisions about what information is to be collected, analyzed, and fed back by the system.

Answering the question "what information should we collect?" is often more difficult than it appears. This is because attention must be given to primary and secondary costs of data collection (Tripodi, Fellin, & Epstein, 1978). Naturally, the program manager wants as much information as he or she can get about youngsters and their families, program interventions and outcomes, and workers. However, the collection, analysis, and feedback of this information has direct material and time costs for research departments, their staff, and program staff to the extent that they are involved in data collection activities. Such involvement also takes program staff away from other forms of program activity, namely, treatment.

Consequently, MIS systems need to contain only those *key* variables related to client need, client change, client welfare and safety, program efforts, effectiveness and efficiency, and worker performance. Here, to avoid the "shot-gun approach," the rule of thumb should be: collect only what you *need* to know and what you have *reason* to want to know, but avoid the temptation to gather information solely on the basis what might be *interesting* to know.

Usually, managers are more knowledgeable than research staff about the clients for whom data are collected, interventions used, and outcomes sought. Consequently, they should be included in discussions about variables and indicators to be included and routinely measured. Moreover, if managers are themselves users of an MIS system, they will be more likely to encourage their staff to participate fully with data collection requirements of the system and to utilize the system in their own day-to-day decision making. This approach promotes the building of accurate and reliable data collection.

At Boysville, a wide spectrum of data is routinely collected. However, what is most helpful for management decision making is information concerning: (1) client history and referral source; (2) characteristics of youth and their families at intake, during treatment and post-release; and (3) treatment services provided and responses to these such as client incidence data. These data are collected and recorded by line staff or obtained directly from clients through self-administered instruments or follow-up interviews.

As a manager who is interested in using this information in programmatic decision making, the first author has been especially eager to ensure that the foregoing information is accurate, reliable, and complete. The result is an increased confidence in decisions that are based, at least in part, on this information. This level of commitment does have its "down side," however. The time involved in developing, debugging, implementing, and generating enough data to utilize such a system can seem terribly long. At Boysville, for example, it took eighteen months to begin data collection. Six years later, we were still adding new elements to the information system such as the educational/academic performance MIS component. Consequently, the manager who wants reliable and accurate data for decision making must accept the fact that system design and implementation is an ongoing endeavor and an incremental process.

UNDERSTANDING THE DATA BASE

The proper use of a management information system for programmatic decision making requires an understanding of what information is *not* collected as well as what is. In addition, it is important to keep in mind *when* and *how* the data are collected. In this way, a program manager can have a fuller, more complete understanding of information provided by the system. An example from Boysville can serve to underscore this point.

Two years ago, Boysville management began considering the inclusion of a treatment program for children who had been sexually abused. Self-reported intake data from BOMIS indicated that 10% of the males in residential treatment at Boysville were sexually abused. This did not square with published studies about the kinds of youths that are in residence at Boysville, nor was it consistent with staff perceptions of the number of times these issues were brought up in the course of treatment. Since the question about sexual abuse was asked at *intake* and related only to *parents* as perpetrators, we suspected that the incidence of sexual abuse actually experienced by youngsters was greatly underreported. A survey of Boysville's group therapists indicated that, in group therapy sessions, over three times as many male youths revealed they had been sexually abused prior to placement as did on their intake forms. And because these revelations have come to light in group sessions, it may be that even this is an understatement of the extent of the problem (Epstein & Grasso, 1990).

This example makes clear that unquestioning reliance placed upon MIS data, no matter how "objective" or "scientific" it looked, would have led to the incorrect inference that prior sexual abuse was not a major issue for Boysville clients. Instead, a critical consideration of when and how the information was collected, the context of the information gathered, as well as a review of the current literature on sexual abuse, led to additional research which supported the inclusion of sexual abuse treatment in the agency program.

Although errors in interpretation are likely to be reduced by early involvement in the development of the system, involvement in the development of the system is not essential. For the previously uninvolved manager, or someone who has joined the organization after the MIS has been developed, a thorough review and critique of the MIS user's manual is helpful as is careful consideration of the context in which data collection takes place. In addition, the insights of other managers who actually use information in their administrative decision making should be sought out.

USAGE OF THE REPORTS

To facilitate using the MIS for programmatic decision making, the first experience with report formats and data feedback should focus on information considered most useful in practice. With this in mind, it is best to concentrate on integrating only one or two initial reports into your practice. The manager should begin by giving attention to the reliability and validity of indicators of program effort and output (Epstein & Tripodi, 1977). These are the performance indicators which best reflect the critical aspects of the program.

Performance indicators can provide key information at a glance and can eliminate reviewing endless pages of computer printouts. Being summary measures, they can be compared across treatment units, and since they can be collected over months or years, performance indicators can facilitate identifying trends and changes over time. But, to give such importance to these data they must be accurate and reliable indicators of what the manager wants to know. In addition, they need to be validated with other data sources and direct observation before they can be relied upon to serve as a basis for decision making.

Once the performance indicators are identified, working closely with MIS staff facilitates getting wanted information. It is important in this process to identify the parts of the data base that represent this information, the time span of the report, and the frequency with which the manager wishes to receive the report. Experience has shown that it is useful to develop, with the programmer, a draft of the intended format, giving him/her a clear idea of how the report should look. It is best to keep the format simple, presenting the data in its most logical arrangement.

Boysville's first BOMIS-generated internal management reports centered on the following performance indicators: type of releases from program, length of stay, and number of incident reports. In addition to serving internal decision making needs, these measures also related to external funding and contractual requirements. For an example of BOMIS's first reports, see Tables 1 and 2.

PLACE DATA IN CONTEXT

After the process of debugging the computer programs and validating the data, and even with the report in hand, the manager is still not in a position to use it for decision making. First it must be carefully studied, questioned, and placed in context. The manager must remember that the data are only **indicators**, not necessarily the diagnosis of or the solution to a problem. The report only tells us *how many*. It must be understood in the light of the practitioner's knowledge of the particular program, its goals, and objectives, and the historical and dynamic relationships among program variables.

The program context from within which the data emerge is terribly important as well. Thus, in residential care, such seemingly unrelated items as recent staff turnover, Christmas holiday home visits, or a particular acting-out of a single youth can drastically change a treatment unit's quarterly data. For this reason, program managers must continue to pay attention to formal and informal feedback from their staff and review positive responses and complaints from youths and families.

Staff turnover as well as external shifts within the environment also can cause problems in integrating data. The report coupled with the manager's wider perspective provides a much more balanced picture of program and staff functioning than does report information.

Michael Austin et al. (1982) contend that MIS reports rarely produce startling, unexpected results since, in most cases, good managers and workers are "in touch" with the results of their program and already have a pretty fair view of the situation. However, Austin and colleagues hold that such information is useful in confirming our suspicions or hunches, or in filling in some knowledge gap of how a program is performing.

Although this is generally correct, data must be collected and analyzed in such a way as to allow for the challenging of the program manager's most cherished practice assumptions, beliefs about clients and workers, and perceptions of the program. By either failing to place information in its proper context or by out-of-hand rejection of the validity of information that refutes expectations, serious errors in interpretation and decision making can result.

Table 1

BOMIS Release Data by Type--Clinton Campus, 1983

Type of Release	Number	Percentage	Length of Stay (Months)
Planned Releases:			
Boysville Release	44	42%	14.3
Administrative Release	26	24%	16.5
TOTAL	70	66%	15.1
Unplanned Terminations:			
Truancy Discharge	16	15%	11.6
Admin. Termination	15	14%	16.1
Court Termination	5	5%	16.8
TOTAL	36	34%	14.2

Table 2

BOMIS Release Data by Group--Clinton Campus, 1983

GROUP	RELEASED YOUTH PLANNED/TERMINATED	PLANNED RELEASES	L.O.S.*	INCIDENT REPORTS PER GROUP
A	7 - 5	58.3%	19.9 mo.	21
B	6 - 4	60.0%	15.2	72
C	7 - 3	70.0%	14.4	57
D	8 - 4	66.7%	13.9	36
E	6 - 2	75.0%	18.3	36
F	9 - 1	90.0%	12.3	36
G	3 - 7	30.0%	16.4	70
H	7 - 5	58.3%	14.8	40
I	8 - 3	72.7%	15.4	39
J	9 - 3	75.0%	13.1	40
TOTAL	70 - 36	66.0%	15.1 mo.	44.7
1984 GOALS	-----	75.0%	13.0 mo.	N/A

*Length of Stay for Planned Releases from program

Another Boysville example illustrates the importance of knowledge about program context when interpreting report data. The example involves the achievement of performance standards within work units. The findings in Table 2 show Group G's program outcomes were noticeably below the campus goal of 75% of youths released. Upon closer review by the manager, it was established that most treatment staff working with the group during the period of time covered in the report had left the agency. Consequently, the staff currently working with Group G were either new to the situation or staff who had remained during very difficult times. In fact, the latter were now chiefly responsible for the markedly improved functioning of the staff team observed by the program manager, but not reflected in the MIS report.

In this context, a critical supervisory response based upon the BOMIS report would have been damaging to the treatment team, to the program manager's relationship with the team, and to the legitimacy of BOMIS. Ultimately, it might have negatively affected future work with the group.

MANAGEMENT ATTITUDE IS CRITICAL

The manner in which the information system's output is shared with staff is critically important. Generally speaking, the agency's management philosophy is reflected in how management information is used. Moreover, the attitude management displays toward MIS and the way they use it will, to a great extent, determine its fate. If the uses of information generated by the system are not integrated with the managerial orientation of the agency, the MIS will be isolated and treated solely as an accountability tool or a device to enforce compliance.

Management information reports *are* a management tool and appropriately so. As such, they are concerned with organizational compliance. But tools can be used to make needed adjustments and improve the functioning of a system, or they can be misused as weapons to beat staff over the head and to dismantle their achievements (Taylor, 1982).

At Boysville, a conscious effort is made to use BOMIS-generated information positively, i.e., to improve the program by information-based, structural change and data-based training. In so doing, Boysville managers utilize the normal management structure and follow official communication channels and flow. First, BOMIS reports are shared, analyzed, and openly discussed with key supervisors and management staff. Next, they are made available to line staff in a similar manner.

To promote utilization of reports, they should be presented to management staff with an explanation of contents, alternative interpretations of findings, program implications, and administrative reaction to them. Reports should be presented to key program supervisors in much the same manner they would be presented to line staff.

Is a report understood? What are staff reactions to it? What questions does the group raise? Feedback and questions raised are frequently suggestive of how line staff will receive a report. This presentation with key staff allows for a test marketing of the report, its findings, and programmatic implications.

To make the best possible use of a report, the meaning of the data and its possible program, practice, and future training implications should be discussed with supervisors. Placing blame on others (youths, families, or staff) should be avoided at all costs. Together, managers and supervisors should determine the what, how, when and where of sharing the report with treatment staff. It is critical to know what key supervisors think of the report and to have their support before presenting a report to line staff.

At Boysville, in addition to considering internal program implications, Regional Directors routinely share program reports with supervisors, presenting program findings in the context of the "bigger agency picture." Thus, MIS data are viewed from the standpoint of contractual obligations, agency goals, and the potential consequences of not meeting performance indicators.

MIS IS A MANAGEMENT TOOL

Wherever possible, MIS reports should be presented to line staff by their immediate supervisors. This underscores the shared value of the MIS and allows the supervisor to intervene as needed. At Boysville, data comparisons concerning different work groups' performance are made in such a way as to protect the confidentiality of each work group. In other words, reports that present comparative data do not name the groups reported. Instead work groups are alphabetically coded, and each supervisor is informed of the code category for his group(s). (See Table 2.) When comparisons are made, they are made between individual work groups and aggregate data for all work groups combined.

Boysville arrived at this practice through hard experience. Originally, MIS reports at Boysville named work groups and indicated their individual performance patterns. As a result, invidious comparisons were made by workers when reports came out without the benefit of a complete contextual understanding of the findings. Thus, Team G in Table 2 was misjudged by other teams whose performance scores were higher because other teams did not link G's performance pattern to problems of staff turnover. This led to hurt feelings and morale problems among those remaining team workers. Since they were carrying a heavier work load than other groups, negative judgements were particularly unjust.

When presenting findings, it is useful to review how the data were gathered and the instruments used. This takes some of the mystery out of these reports. If the findings are positive, the supervisor should give credit and acknowledgment for a job well done. Performance goals for the next report period should be restated and the continued assistance of staff requested.

If the report shows poor performance, a sympathetic ear and kind firmness are required. More than likely, staff already know there are performance problems, and they may be defensive about the causes. They may challenge the validity of measures or the accuracy of data. These challenges need to be taken seriously. If they are groundless, however, there needs to be a frank and open discussion of the problems, their causes and ways to remediate them. Performance goals need to be restated, and support and encouragement provided. Additional training may be needed.

Here again, a punitive response is dysfunctional. There is no easier way to kill a management information system than to use it against staff. Workers quickly learn to sabotage a punitive system through non-compliance in data-collection, falsification of data and/or non-utilization (Grasso & Epstein, 1987). As a result, program, workers, and clients suffer.

Regardless of whether the report is good or bad news, the presenter should be objective in his or her use of language, not exaggerating positives or negatives. In a feedback meeting, findings should be presented concisely and efficiently so that time is left for consideration of program and practice implications. Under a supervisor's guidance, negative findings can be the start of a very positive process of group problem-solving, skills development, and cohesion building among team members.

MONITOR CHANGES OVER TIME

Once reports have been designed, produced, and shared, their impact needs to be monitored. Depending on the nature of the report, managers may want to monitor resulting changes monthly or quarterly. In child care agencies such as Boysville, a considerable time lag is quite common between monitored events and the produced report. Naturally, the shorter the time lag the better. For the MIS report to be useful, it must allow for: (1) timely review; (2) specific identification of problem areas; (3) suggestions about ways to solve problems; and (4) ongoing monitoring and evaluation of change efforts (Young, 1978).

At Boysville, most BOMIS program reports are issued quarterly, with year-to-date summaries likewise issued for each quarter. Program managers regularly share data with their staff teams, discuss related implications as necessary, and engage in problem-solving using management-by-objectives-like goal achievement procedures. Regional directors meet with each team annually to review performance and reinforce performance goals and their attainment.

Quarterly updates and annual reviews follow a routine set of procedures that include: (1) analysis and critical questioning of the findings; (2) discussion of the report and its implications with key supervisors; and (3) discussion of the report and its implications for line staff. For two reasons, it is particularly important that this progression be followed each time reports are issued. First, there will always be staff turnover in child care programs. New staff will be unfamiliar with the report and the agency's purpose and way of using the report. Even if staff turnover has been minimal, a three-month gap between reports leaves considerable time for forgetting the report's content and intent. Contexts need to be updated.

As a result, each quarter presents the program manager with the opportunity and the necessity of reteaching the report format, its purpose and its implications. Second, a regular quarterly review process provides managers with an opportunity to reinforce the program's commitment to using MIS data to *improve* program quality and effectiveness, as opposed to serving accountability needs alone.

Once the report format is tested and refined and staff become familiar with its content and uses, it can be employed regularly. Once established, it should only be necessary to change the report dates, and include past year/quarter data as the report gains a history.

Table 3 is an example of a report format built upon earlier reports. Wherever possible, key performance indicators must be maintained. Major changes in performance indicators will cause confusion among staff and negate possible comparisons with the previous year's performance.

Once basic reports are institutionalized, new report formats can fill in the wider picture of child care programming. While initial performance indicators focused on what you *must* know as a manager, subsequent reports can begin to address more refined performance indicators that you now want to know, and perhaps can even center on more interesting questions about clients and their responses to treatment. As BOMIS evolved, later reports were intended to answer questions that emerged from discussions of earlier reports. These questions concerned how to

Table 3

BOMIS Release Data by Year 1983-1987

YEAR	RELEASED YOUTH PLANNED/TERMINATED	PLANNED RELEASES	L.O.S.*	INCIDENT REPORTS PER GROUP
1983	70 - 36	66.0%	15.1 mo.	44.7
1984	86 - 36	70.5%	14.8	36.2
1985	89 - 37	70.6%	13.1	51.3
1986	87 - 26	77.0%	13.6	40.6
1987	96 - 32	75.0%	14.3	52.5
GOAL for 1988	------	75.0%	12.0 mo.	35.0

*Length of Stay for Planned Releases from program

improve our current treatment program or areas needing additional service provision.

For example, Tables 1, 2, and 3 all report on youths released from the campus-based residential program. Findings indicate that some treatment teams maintained higher release rates while performing below standard on internal measures such as incident reports, length of stay, or quality of group culture. These inconsistent findings naturally raised question about the quality and strength of releases from these treatment teams. Did youths from the groups with high release rates and low internal performance measures have as successful adjustments in the community as those from groups where the findings were more consistent? Did released youths with longer lengths of stay better maintain the treatment gains? Did youths from the groups with more positive group cultures adjust better post-release, irrespective of their length of stay?

Since BOMIS routinely collects follow-up data concerning post-placement adjustment at 3 months, 12 months, and 18 months, MIS staff recently took the opportunity to develop a Post-Placement Adjustment Survey Scale. This scale measures youth adjustment to the community by looking at school and work performance, living situation, and frequency of police contact. This scale will serve as a basis of a new report format that will indicate success of post-placement adjustment of youths who are treated by different teams and will assist in answering the questions detailed above.

"MIS"-BASED DECISION MAKING

Throughout this article, the point has been made that one of the primary purposes of BOMIS has been to inform and improve programmatic decision making. At Boysville, emphasis is placed on using management information to facilitate service delivery and increase the effectiveness and efficiency of programs. In this context, performance statistics are viewed as only indicators rather than as ends in themselves. Thus, Boysville's operating assumption is that if the treatment program is improved, performance indicators will reflect these changes (Grasso & Epstein, 1987).

This assumption has not been universally embraced over the course of BOMIS's development. For example, in the early history of BOMIS, one Regional Director focused his attention solely on improving outcome statistics as though they were ends-in-themselves. Accordingly, he conveyed the message to his subordinates that he wanted performance data to improve without detailing how. Program Supervisors applied this perspective in a variety of ways, but with equally disastrous effects.

Some began blaming staff and threatened punitive action if statistics did not improve. Others blamed client intake procedures and suggested that more difficult youths be rejected by Boysville. A few resorted to falsification of data.

As a result, not only did the treatment program fail to improve, but the image of BOMIS was undermined at these sites. Two years later, program staff in this region are just beginning to recognize the positive uses of BOMIS. Thus, a narrow, cynical, and/or punitive attitude towards the use of MIS by program administration can cause serious harm to the service program as well as to the information system itself.

On a more positive note, BOMIS-generated information has been quite helpful in making three types of programmatic decisions. The first involves a change in program activities. This might involve changes of long-standing practices that were never before questioned. So, for example, an analysis of the monthly distribution of Incident Reports indicated a sharp increase after the Christmas holiday home visits. These data helped influence Boysville's administration to change the agency's policy of sending nearly every youth home for a five-day visit during the holiday season. Now, Christmas home visits are contingent on treatment considerations and youth/family readiness.

A second type of decision that has been positively influenced by BOMIS involves services related to staff training and program consultation. In general, BOMIS has shown that poor outcome statistics are not the result of weak staff commitment, but rather a consequence of limited staff skills. In fact, staff are often working harder in those units which have less favorable outcomes. By considering these statistics as indicators of needed training and/or consultation and providing these services to staff, program quality and performance outcomes have been improved. Thus, for example, staff training for more effective dealing with "acting out" youths has improved program quality and reduced the number of "incidents" reported.

Finally, BOMIS has been used to study changes in the client population and/or unmet client needs. One example of this kind of programmatic change involves the decision to initiate a sexual abuse treatment program for youths and their families as cited earlier. Information generated by BOMIS supports the provision of this new form of treatment, will help specify its focus, and will be used to evaluate its effectiveness.

CONCLUSIONS

This paper has made the case that MIS data can be used to improve program quality as well as satisfy accountability requirements. Practice principles for the effective use of management information data in pro-grammatic decision making were articulated. Specific examples of the application of these principles at Boysville were presented. BOMIS is now six years old. However, it is just beginning to demonstrate its considerable potential for improving service effectiveness and efficiency. As a conse-quence, line staff and program managers alike are beginning to see how they, and the children and families they serve, can benefit from the in-formation BOMIS routinely provides.

REFERENCES

Austin, M. J., et al. (1982). *Evaluating your agency's programs.* Beverly Hills, CA.: Sage Human Services.

Bielawski, B., & Epstein, I. (1984). Using program stabilization: An extension of the differential evaluation model. *Administration in Social Work, 8,* 13-23.

Epstein, I., & Grasso, A. (1990). Using agency based available information to further practice innovation. In H. Weissman (Ed.), *Serious play: Creativity and innovation in social work.* New York: NASW Press.

Epstein, I., & Tripodi, T. (1977). *Research techniques for program planning, monitoring, and evaluation.* New York: Columbia University Press.

Grasso, A. J., & Epstein, I. (1987). Management by measurement: Organizational dilemmas and opportunities. *Administration in Social Work, 11,* 89-100.

Grasso, A. J., & Epstein, I. (1989). The Boysville experience: Integrating practice decision making, program evaluation, and management information. *Computers in Human Services, 4,* 85-95.

Grasso, A. J., Epstein, I., & Tripodi, T. (1988). Agency-based research utilization in a residential child care setting. *Adminstration in Social Work, 12,* 61-80.

Hoshino, G. (1978). Social services: The problem of accountability. In S. Slavin (Ed.), *Social administration: The management of the social services.* New York: The Haworth Press, Inc.

Patti, R., & Austin, M. J. (1977). Socializing the direct-service practitioner in ways of supervisory management. *Administration in Social Work, 1,* 273-80.

Taylor, J. B. (1982). *Using microcomputers in social agencies.* Beverly Hills, CA: Sage Human Services.

Tripodi, T., Fellin, P., & Epstein, I. (1978). *Differential social program evaluation.* Itasca, IL: Peacock Press.

Weber, R. E., & Polansky, N. A. (1975). Evaluation. *Social work research.* Chicago, IL: University of Chicago Press.

Young, D. W. (1978). Management information systems in child care: An agency experience. In S. Slavin (Ed.), *Social administration: The management of the social services.* New York: The Haworth Press, Inc.

Clinical Assessment and Program Evaluation in the Boysville Pastoral Ministry Program

Eugene Hausmann
Irwin Epstein

ABSTRACT. Researchers involved in the scientific study of religion have recently developed a number of research instruments that attempt to measure psychological and sociological dimensions of spirituality. The Boysville pastoral ministry program routinely employs computerized information concerning clients' religious attitudes, beliefs, and practices in serving the spiritual needs of its clients while in placement and in supporting positive treatment outcomes post-release. This paper enumerates clinical and programmatic uses of this data base and suggests some basic research questions that might also be explored through its use.

People do not generally think of pastoral ministry programs in conjunction with research and/or management information systems. One reason

Eugene Hausmann is affiliated with Boysville of Michigan, 8744 Clinton-Macon Road, Clinton, MI 49236. Irwin Epstein is affiliated with the School of Social Work, Hunter College, City University of New York, 129 East 79th Street, New York, NY 10021.

[Haworth co-indexing entry note]: "Clinical Assessment and Program Evaluation in the Boysville Pastoral Ministry Program." Hausmann, Eugene, and Irwin Epstein. Co-published simultaneously in *Child & Youth Services,* (The Haworth Press, Inc.) Vol. 16, No. 1, 1993, pp. 95-106; and: *Information Systems in Child, Youth, and Family Agencies: Planning, Implementation, and Service Enhancement* (ed: Anthony J. Grasso, and Irwin Epstein) The Haworth Press, Inc., 1993, pp. 95-106. Multiple copies of this article/chapter may be purchased from The Haworth Document Delivery Center. Call 1-800-3-HAWORTH (1-800-342-9678) between 9:00 - 5:00 (EST) and ask for DOCUMENT DELIVERY CENTER.

for this is the common belief that spiritual development and interventions that facilitate this development are unmeasurable. Despite these popular beliefs, over the past two decades, researchers involved in the scientific study of religion have developed a number of research instruments that tap the psychological and sociological dimensions of spirituality (Robinson & Shaver, 1973).

More recently, applied researchers have begun to explore the impacts of pastoral ministry on spiritual development as well as physical health. For example, McSherry (1984) refers to several recent studies that correlate pastoral care and medical interventions with patient recovery. These research efforts are aimed at demonstrating the cost-effectiveness of chaplaincy in hospital settings. In McSherry's words, "This new objectification moves modern chaplaincy and inpatient spiritual health into the realm of health and medical science, not just an intuitive art in health care" (p. 2).

Not surprisingly, critics of this "new objectification" of spirituality express fear that the use of computers and quantitative measures of pastoral interventions and outcomes will destroy human aspects of the relationship between those giving and those receiving religious services. This opposition to computerization is likely to be held even more strongly in social service organizations where religious and social work practitioners alike harbor anti-research sentiments. Perhaps one indicator of this is that there are no published studies describing the use of computers and management information data in a pastoral ministry program in a social work agency.

This article describes the Boysville pastoral ministry program which routinely employs computers and management information data concerning clients' religious attitudes, beliefs, and practices. Beginning with a discussion of the place of pastoral ministry in the Boysville treatment program, the article goes on to enumerate uses of the Religion Survey for client assessment and program planning and evaluation. It concludes with a consideration of future clinical and research issues that can be explored through this innovative program.

Although the impetus for its initiation was an overwhelming caseload size, the routine use of computerized religious information in Boysville's pastoral ministry program was found to enhance the quality, effectiveness, and efficiency of religious interventions.

PASTORAL MINISTRY AT BOYSVILLE OF MICHIGAN

In residential child care agencies, both public and private, increasingly tight budgets, emphasis on secular treatment technologies, and church-

and-state concerns limit the extent to which pastoral ministry programs are supported and integrated into overall treatment programs. When they exist at all, pastoral ministry programs are limited in size and scope and treated as extraneous to the primary treatment core and process.

By contrast, the Boysville Pastoral Ministry Program (PMP) is considered an integral part of Boysville's treatment program. As such, it is intended to provide diagnostic assessment, treatment planning, and treatment interventions based on information concerning the spirituality of individual youths in placement and their families. Thus, at Boysville, the Pastoral Minister functions as a resource to treatment teams that are themselves responsible for achieving overall treatment goals of the agency.

In this way, the Boysville program differs markedly from other treatment programs which exclude the spiritual dimension from the treatment process and which relegate religion to an honorable but peripheral role in the agency. As in other agencies, however, budget priorities and constraints limit the amount of material and staff resources allocated to this function. Historically, and despite its decentralization, Boysville has had only one chaplain serving all sites with a caseload of at least 120 youths on the main campus alone.

More recently, with rapid program expansion the caseload increased to 250. Moreover, because composition of caseloads is constantly changing through existing client discharge and new client entry, caseloads of such magnitude make individualized, treatment-oriented ministry virtually impossible.

One response the agency took to this increase in client census was to hire an additional chaplain. Another was the adoption of a computerized process of spiritual information gathering, analysis, and dissemination for purposes of diagnostic assessment. The remaining portion of this paper describes the basic elements of PMP's MIS program, its current uses and future possibilities. Specific attention is given to ways in which this program enriches the treatment process as well as the quality of pastoral care offered to Boysville youths and their families.

ADMINISTRATION OF THE YOUTH RELIGION SURVEY

Three years ago, PMP implemented a Youth Religion Survey (YRS) at Boysville to all incoming clients. In addition to basic religious and demographic information, the survey profiles religious beliefs, values, interests, and past experiences of youngsters and quantifies them along ten different dimensions. These dimensions, based on instruments developed by Benson (1982), Rohrbach and Jessor (1975), and Batson (1982), include:

1. Positive God Concept, i.e., the extent to which the subject's perception of God is nurturing and unconditionally loving;
2. Social Spirituality, i.e., the extent to which the subject's spirituality involves concern for other human beings;
3. Ritual Religiosity, i.e., the subject's past experience in prayer and worship;
4. Ideological Religiosity, i.e., the degree to which the subject is committed to a creed;
5. Consequential Religiosity, i.e., the degree to which the subject's faith affects his/her daily life decisions;
6. Experiential Religiosity, i.e., the frequency of personal religious experience reported by the subject;
7. Religious Interest, i.e., the degree to which the subject indicates interest in church attendance and other religious activities;
8. Family Religiosity, i.e., the youth's perception of how important religion is to the parents;
9. Religiosity Dissonance, i.e., the difference between the youth's religiosity score and the Family Religiosity score (indicating how much religion may be at issue in family relationships);
10. Tradition Strength, i.e., an attempt to measure how strong is the actual church involvement in the family background.

In addition to the above, A-COPES and F-COPES Spiritual Support scores (McCubbin & Thompson, 1987) are incorporated into the reports. These scores measure how much support the youth (A-COPES) and family (F-COPES) experience from church resources in times of crisis. In addition, they serve as a cross-check for our religiosity scores.

The foregoing information is gathered by means of a 47-item, self-administered questionnaire that takes approximately 1/2 hour to complete. It is given to youngsters at intake along with other clinical diagnostic instruments which measure social, psychological, educational, and family dimensions. In addition, students are asked to indicate their perceptions of their parents' religiosity. This makes possible computation of a Religious Dissonance Scale which indicates the degree of difference between the youth's religiosity and that of his family. Finally, members of the PMP conduct one-to-one, qualitative interviews with incoming youths.

Once the information is collected, a secretary at the particular Boysville location enters the data into a pre-programmed software package that prints out a one-page narrative that is based upon the religious information collected. Three examples of client religious profiles are presented next.

Perhaps the most common religious profile of Boysville youth is that reflected in Figure 1. The family has a traditional set of attitudes and

FIGURE 1

Sample Profile #1

BOYSVILLE OF MICHIGAN   SPIRITUAL ASSESSMENT   RC01

CASE #:   NAME:

STAY #:   DATE OF BIRTH: GRADE:

SITE #:   GROUP: ESTIMATED RELEASE MONTH:

ESTIMATED DESTINATION AT RELEASE: ZIP:

The youth named above is a member of the Baptist tradition. This youth perceives the mother's religion as slightly important to her and the father's religion as not important to him. The religion topic is never discussed in the family.

The youth believes that God exists, believes that Jesus was the Son of God and believes that the Bible is the Word of God.

Prior to placement, the youth attended church less than once a month and prayed 2-3 times a week. She attended youth group meetings less than once a month and has had 5-7 years experience in Religious Education programs. The youth states some interest in church.

While in placement, this youth states much interest in attending a retreat and some interest in joining a youth group. If the youth joined a group, the following characteristics would be of interest: other Boysville graduates present, serious discussions, helping needy people, praying together and fun things. The youth has had the following religious experiences: Being saved.

The youth is interested in discussing the following spiritual events: Baptism and Bible Study.

beliefs, but has not been significantly involved in church activities; the youth professes belief in basic Christian doctrines, but has had involvement in church only as a child and more recently has drifted away from participation. Though the youth has not been religiously involved recently, she expresses interest in some of the ministry opportunities in the Boysville program.

Figure 2 illustrates another common pattern, that of the "unbeliever."

FIGURE 2

Sample Profile #2

```
BOYSVILLE OF MICHIGAN        SPIRITUAL ASSESSMENT              RC01

CASE #:                 NAME:

STAY #:                 DATE OF BIRTH:            GRADE:

SITE #:       GROUP:                 ESTIMATED RELEASE MONTH:

ESTIMATED DESTINATION AT RELEASE:                    ZIP:
```

The youth named above is a member of the Roman Catholic tradition. This youth perceives his mother's religion as important to her and the father's religion as slightly important to him. The religion topic is never discussed in the family.

The youth doesn't thins that God exists, is uncertain about who Jesus is and believes that the BIBLE is a famous moral book.

Prior to his placement, the youth never attended church services and prayed less than once a week. He never attended youth group meetings and has had 0-1 year experience in Religious Education programs. The youth states uncertain interest in church.

While in placement, this youth states no interest in attending a retreat and uncertain interest in joining a youth group. If the youth joined a group, the following characteristics would be of interest: other Boysville graduates present, helping needy people and doing fun things. The youth has had the following religious experiences: receiving communion. The youth is not interested in discussing any spiritual events.

These youths are disinterested at best, perhaps even hostile to anything religious. Typically, unbelievers have been either overloaded with religion by an overzealous parent or not exposed at all to religion during childhood. Remarkably, however, it is not unusual for this type of youth to express interest in some ministry activities.

Figure 3 profiles a religious "enthusiast." This type of youth has been significantly involved in church activities until s/he was taken out of the home and continues to be interested in almost every ministry activity in Boysville. What is atypical in this particular example is the youth's expressed uncertainty regarding basic Christian beliefs.

At Boysville, these narratives are routinely inserted into the record of each youngster and serve as part of his/her social history as psycho-social assessment. As such, it becomes part of the information base for a comprehensive, individualized, interdisciplinary treatment plan.

In addition, the religious data collected serve as a "before" measure for clinical and program evaluation. This is possible since the same instrument is routinely administered after a youngster is in placement eight months and upon discharge from the program.

TREATMENT PLAN: GOALS AND INTERVENTIONS

The foregoing assessment summaries (and their more detailed quantitative profiles) are used by the PMP as a basis for pastoral treatment planning, setting of treatment goals, and planning interventions to work toward the goals. This enables the PMP to tailor the ministry to the needs and interests of each youth and family. To illustrate this process, we return to our three case examples.

The first case is typical of about 60% of Boysville's client population. This youth participated minimally in church prior to placement, yet shows interest in some religious events. In this case a pastoral ministry goal would be to establish membership in a youth group near her home prior to release from the program. She is most interested in three interventions: retreat experience, Bible study, and baptism. The long range plan should include participation on a Boysville retreat and, later in her program, on a retreat with an outside youth group, preferably a group from her home neighborhood.

Bible study sessions focused on the baptism theme could begin early in the program. The study would highlight an aspect of the baptism event which involves an ongoing relationship with a supportive faith community. If she wishes to follow up on the study and the retreats, then she may be ready for additional interventions involving meeting and selecting a group

FIGURE 3

Sample Profile #3

BOYSVILLE OF MICHIGAN   SPIRITUAL ASSESSMENT   RC01

CASE #:   NAME:

STAY #:   DATE OF BIRTH: GRADE:

SITE #:   GROUP: ESTIMATED RELEASE MONTH:

ESTIMATED DESTINATION AT RELEASE: ZIP:

The youth named above is a member of the Methodist tradition. This youth perceives the mother's religion as extremely important to her and the father's religion as unknown. The religion topic is discussed in the family about once a week.

The youth is not sure that God exists, is uncertain about who Jesus is and is unclear as to the meaning of the Bible.

Prior to placement, the youth attended church services once a week or more and prayed 2-3 times a week. He attended youth group meetings about once a week and has had more than 10 years of Religious Education. The youth is very interested in church.

While in placement, this youth is very interested in attending a retreat and in membership in a youth group. The following characteristics would be of interest: other Boysville graduates present, serious discussions, helping needy people, praying together and doing fun things. The youth has had the following religious experiences: Baptism and Communion. The youth is interested in discussing the following spiritual events: Baptism, Confirmation, Being Saved and Bible Study.

that she may wish to join and receiving additional preparations for baptism from that pastor or a representative.

The second case, the "unbeliever," is typical of about 15% of Boysville youth. If the youngster expresses disbelief because s/he has never been exposed to religion, there is a good chance the religious interest score may still be high, reflecting curiosity. However, in this case, there is no interest expressed, indicating a rejection of religion as well as disbelief. An appropriate treatment plan for this youth would involve avoiding the topic of religion altogether, unless the youth initiates the discussion.

In the latter event, the goal would be to achieve an attitude of openness in the youth to explore spiritual issues, but the interventions involved providing him/her with lots of space and time to come to answer, in his/her own way, personal questions about life, death, and existence.

The third case, the active church member, is typical of about 25% of Boysville's client population. The pastoral goal is likely to involve maintaining or improving the youth's relationship with God and the Church. Key to achieving this goal is the continuing involvement of the pastor or pastoral representative and supportive church members (preferably peers). This youth is probably at or near the age of Confirmation and is expressing interest.

Key interventions include arranging ongoing sessions with the family's church to prepare the youth for the Confirmation event and maintaining relationships in the church peer group. Ideally, the final event in the plan would be the celebration of Confirmation by family members with both Boysville and church peers witnessing.

IMPACT OF THE COMPUTERIZED MINISTRY PROGRAM

Introduction of a computerized information system for PMP has had a positive impact on Boysville at several different levels. First, it has expanded the potential clinical impact of PMP beyond the main campus where the chaplain has traditionally had his office. Now, the entire agency can be served. Before its introduction, it was virtually impossible for the chaplain to do anything but group programming at satellite locations. Now, he can carry on meaningful treatment planning with clinical staff at every Boysville location.

The following are process notes that serve to illustrate an individualized planning session that took place between a treatment worker and the chaplain:

Chaplain: We're having a retreat day next month for youths and their families on the theme of forgiveness of family hurts. Based on the Youth Religion Survey I noticed that three of the families you are working with scored high on perceived religiosity. They might be interested in such a program to improve relationships with their youngsters.

Family Worker: Sounds good. To which families are you referring?

Chaplain: Families A, B, and C.

Family Worker: Interesting. A and C make sense based on what I've seen of them, but I never would have expected the Bs to be religious.

Chaplain: Well, they do score high. Why don't you approach them about participating and see what they say?

Family Worker: O.K., but now that you mention it I'm surprised that the D family is not on your list.

Chaplain: Well, they did score high on religiosity, but they are Jehovah's Witnesses and will not participate in an interdenominational religious retreat. It's against their religious beliefs.

The foregoing dialogue between family worker and chaplain not only describes an actual example of how family religiosity scores are used in deciding who should be invited to the retreat, but illustrates as well some of the underlying principles followed in the implementation of the computerized program. First, there is a true dialogue between treatment and pastoral ministry staff so that they engage in treatment planning as a team. Second, neither relies solely on the computer scores in making decisions. Instead, they consider these in the context of what they know about the beliefs of different religious groups. Finally, participation in this religious program for clients and their families is entirely voluntary for all concerned. Thus, in some highly dissonant families parents may participate without their children. In others, where the children are more religious than their parents, the opposite is true.

Even more refined judgments about youth participation might involve consideration of profiles based upon scores on different scales such as Religious Interest versus Ideological Religiosity. Irrespective of the level of refinement achieved, this kind of team planning could not have taken place prior to implementation of the computerized program.

A second way in which the computerized information system has enriched pastoral practice at Boysville is by making possible the assessment of individual spiritual growth while youngsters are in the program. Thus, by considering individual differences between youngster's scores at intake, after 8 months, and upon discharge it is possible to assess the impact of religious interventions on individual clients. This also makes possible discharge planning that takes into account the religious interests and needs of youngsters who are re-entering the community.

In doing so, PMP staff make use of a *Transition Information Report* and a *Computerized Directory of Youth Groups.* The former provides key information about the religious interests, release date and destination of youth scheduled for release. The latter contains information on approximately 600 groups available to youth throughout the service area. Most of these are church-based, and the directory provides information about denomination, location, types of activities, program contact persons, etc. By matching information from the Transition Report with information from the directory, effective referrals can be made for post-release religious involvement.

In addition, aggregation of spiritual change scores will allow Boysville management and administrative staff to do pastoral treatment team and/or total pastoral program evaluation. It is necessary to remember, however, that in doing individual treatment planning and individual evaluation, or treatment team and total program evaluations, a true dialogue must take place between PMP and clinical staff on the one hand and between PMP staff and program directors on the other.

In each of these instances, computer output should never be the only source of relevant "data." Instead, qualitative observation, other quantitative MIS data, professional judgment, and common sense are all integral elements in client, team, and program evaluation.

DIRECTIONS FOR FUTURE STUDY AND PROGRAM EXPANSION

Now that PMP has begun collecting information on the religious attitudes, beliefs, and practices of our clients, we can begin to address the following basic research questions:

1. What are the religious attitudes, beliefs, and practices of children in care? How do these differ from non-clinical populations? Do children in care become more like their non-clinical counterparts in the course of treatment?
2. How are other background characteristics of children in care (e.g., race, age, adjudications, offense categories, etc.) associated with religious attitudes, beliefs, and practices?

From the standpoint of program evaluation however, a set of interdisciplinary treatment questions now can be addressed. These include the following:

1. How are religious beliefs, attitudes, and practices measured at intake associated with non-religious treatment outputs and outcomes?
2. How do changes in religious beliefs, attitudes, and practices while in the program affect non-religious treatment outputs and outcomes?
3. How are religious treatment interventions related to non-religious treatment outputs and outcomes?
4. What is the relationship between religious and non-religious treatment intervention patterns?
5. Do religious and non-religious interventions have an additive effect, serve as functional equivalents, or undermine each other in the production of treatment outputs and outcomes?
6. How are differences in youth background characteristics associated with the foregoing questions?

Because BOMIS is an integrated, interactive data system, once the Youth Religious Survey data are read into it, research staff will be able to answer these important questions. This is planned for the near future. In the meantime, the existing computerized Youth Religious Survey and the reports and uses it has already generated have contributed substantially to the scope, effectiveness, and efficiency of Boysville's pastoral services to children and their families.

REFERENCES

Batson, C. D. (1982). *Religious experience: A sociological/psychological perspective.* New York: Oxford University Press.

Benson, P. L. (1982). *Early adolescents and their parents: A national survey.* Minneapolis: Search Institute.

McCubbin, H. I., & Thompson, A. I. (1987). *Family assessment inventories.* Madison: University of Wisconsin.

McSherry, E. (1984). *Pastoral care departments in the DRG-era: New accountability allows overall medical cost savings.* Paper presented at the National Walter Reed Medical Conference, Washington, DC.

Robinson, J., & Shaver, P. (1973). *Measures of social psychological attitudes.* Ann Arbor: Institute of Social Research.

Rohrback, J., & Jessor, R. (1975). Religiosity in youth: A personal control against deviant behavior. *Journal of Personality,* March, 136-155.

Management Information Systems and External Policy Advocacy: The Boysville Length of Stay Study

Edward J. Overstreet
Anthony J. Grasso
Irwin Epstein

ABSTRACT. In an effort to cut child care costs, the Michigan Department of Social Services proposed a reduced length of stay policy for children in placement. Their proposal was to favor agencies with shorter lengths of stay in funding decisions. This paper describes how BOMIS data concerning Boysville client length of stay and its relation to client outcomes was used to successfully challenge a potentially harmful state policy.

In 1984, in an effort to cut residential child care costs, the Michigan Department of Social Services (MDSS) proposed that future residential

Edward J. Overstreet is Associate Executive Director, Boysville of Michigan, 8744 Clinton-Macon Road, Clinton, MI 49236. Anthony J. Grasso is Director, School of Social Work, University of Nevada at Las Vegas, 4505 Maryland Parkway, Las Vegas, NV 89154-5032. Irwin Epstein is affiliated with the School of Social Work, Hunter College, City University of New York, 129 East 79th Street, New York, NY 10021.

[Haworth co-indexing entry note]: "Management Information Systems and External Policy Advocacy: The Boysville Length of Stay Study." Overstreet, Edward J., Anthony J. Grasso, and Irwin Epstein. Co-published simultaneously in *Child & Youth Services*, (The Haworth Press, Inc.) Vol. 16, No. 1, 1993, pp. 107-122; and: *Information Systems in Child, Youth, and Family Agencies: Planning, Implementation, and Service Enhancement* (ed: Anthony J. Grasso, and Irwin Epstein) The Haworth Press, Inc., 1993, pp. 107-122. Multiple copies of this article/chapter may be purchased from The Haworth Document Delivery Center. Call 1-800-3-HAWORTH (1-800-342-9678) between 9:00 - 5:00 (EST) and ask for DOCUMENT DELIVERY CENTER.

107

child care funding be linked to client length of stay. The authors of this paper criticized the MDSS study from which this policy was generated claiming it was based upon faulty assumptions and flawed methodology. As a consequence, we argued that policy implications derived from that study were unsound and potentially harmful to residential child care agencies and to the children they serve.

This article describes how a more methodologically robust study of client length of stay using readily available BOMIS-generated data made it possible to alter a potentially harmful state policy. Although there are other child welfare policy, program, and practice ramifications associated with length of stay, the article is intended to illustrate the way BOMIS data were used to refute the assumptions, findings, and policy implications of the MDSS study.

From a methodological standpoint, this article presents a qualitative case study based on quantitative data. This apparent contradiction is resolved when it is explained that the article illustrates how BOMIS-generated, quantitative data concerning Boysville's clients were used by its executive staff to successfully alter poorly designed accountability standards put forth by the State of Michigan. The story is told in the form of an historical narrative.

More generally, this article describes how an integrated information system such as BOMIS can be employed by agency executives for the purpose of external policy advocacy. The first portion of the article details political and fiscal climates prevailing in Michigan in the late 70s and early 80s. The remainder presents some of the reasoning, quantitative data, and policy analysis employed by Boysville administrators in cooperation with executives from other Michigan residential child care agencies to counter the direction of state policy.

THE FISCAL AND POLITICAL CLIMATE

In the late 70s and early 80s, economic conditions and a conservative administration caused federal policy to place increasing pressure on human service organizations to contain costs (Patti, 1983). Programs whose existence had historically gone unquestioned found themselves being asked to justify financial expenditures in relationship to service effectiveness. Residential care facilities experienced this cost containment effort in the form of pressure to reduce client length of stay.

By the early 1980s, reduction of length of stay had become a constant and nagging theme, for child welfare administrators in particular, and human service agency administrators in general. In Michigan, these pressures became most apparent in 1983, when Governor Blanchard committed himself to trying to balance his state budget. In an effort to achieve this political goal, he increased the state income tax, promising that once the budget was balanced, the tax would be reduced and the burden for taxpayers relieved.

In addition to raising taxes, Blanchard gave the Director of Social Services, Agnes Mansour, the task of finding new ways to reduce costs in the MDSS budget. As for residential child care, her task was made all the more difficult by rapidly increasing demand for residential child care in the state. The following excerpt taken from a study conducted by MDSS reflects the conflicting priorities with which state child welfare policymakers were charged at the time:

> The State Department of Social Services needs to find a way to continue or expand service delivery for residential care, while at the same time reducing or at least not increasing costs for residential care. (Cartwright, 1982)

By 1985, rising costs in residential care in Michigan placed additional strain on the MDSS's efforts to provide needed services to children and their families. In a meeting in November, 1985, Roger Lewis, the Deputy Director of the Michigan Office of Children and Youth Services, stated that the Department of Social Services had to deal with approximately 1,000 new commitments each year. With the average cost of services reaching about $36,000 annually for each client coming into care, the addition of 1,000 new commitments each year represented an enormous additional financial burden for an already beleaguered Department of Social Services. This problem was intensified by the fact that the preceding five years had seen a dramatic reduction in state revenues as a result of job loss in the auto industry. Ultimately, the Department considered shortening length of stay in residential child care settings so as to reduce child welfare costs.

USING BOMIS FOR PUBLIC POLICY ADVOCACY

The remainder of this article presents a case illustration of how a quantitative study, based upon BOMIS data, was used to demonstrate to MDSS that basing state funding priorities primarily upon agency length of stay statistics was a potentially destructive policy course. In addition, the article makes the point that the uses of integrated information systems such as BOMIS are not restricted to internal programmatic decision making or to external accountability purposes, but can be applied to issues of external policy advocacy as well. Ultimately, of course, all three sets of issues are linked, since state policy regarding residential child care funding and accountability influences internal decision making about the quality and quantity of care.

MDSS LENGTH OF STAY STUDY

In 1982, MDSS conducted its own length of stay study based upon the following underlying intent:

> To assure the best use of available dollars, the Department is develop-ing additional capabilities for operating, and/or contracting for, only those programs which provide the highest priority services and which do it well at the lowest overall cost. This study of children's residential services in Michigan was done to aid in developing these capabilities. (Cartwright, 1982)

Based upon accountability data from agencies throughout the state, the MDSS length of stay study found marked differences in average length of stay in different residential child care agencies. In addition, it discovered a U-shaped, bi-modal relationship between client length of stay and "posi-tive program outcomes." The latter term means a positive disposition for the client three months after program termination. In other words, many clients were in "less restrictive" placements three months after discharge following relatively short lengths of stay (i.e., 7 months). An equally high proportion had such positive program outcomes following relatively long lengths of stay (i.e., 16 months). In the MDSS study, no data were pro-vided on client status at time of program termination to indicate whether positive program outcomes were associated with post-discharge adjust-ment. Inferring cost saving implications from this study, MDSS policy-makers proposed the following new guidelines for purchase of service contracts. Performance objectives linked to length of stay would be ap-plied to all residential child care agencies in the state, and funding priority would be given to agencies that reported the shortest average lengths of stay. The proposed formula applied a general, statistical performance stan-dard or norm to all agencies based on the midpoint between the two peaks in the state's data (i.e., 11.5 months).

Upon release of this report, Boysville's executive staff became concerned. The program and practice implications of a policy that simply rewarded those agencies with shortest average length of stay raised serious treatment-related questions. What impact would this policy have on quality of care? Would it foster premature release of youngsters whose treatment might appropriately exceed the statistical norm? Would clients who were prematurely released enter the "revolving door" post-release recidivism? Would the state save money at the expense of state wards? Ultimately, would premature release and the consequent recidivism cost the state even more?

Boysville research staff, familiar with the BOMIS data concerning client length of stay, were also troubled by assumptions contained within and research methodology employed in the MDSS study. They questioned, for example, the assumption of the MDSS study that "positive program outcome" (i.e., client status three months post-discharge) was causally linked to length of stay. Instead, their program experience and research data suggested that length of stay was simply a correlate of client discharge status. In other words, length of stay was simply an "indicator" of the type of client discharge.

Moreover, the state made the assumption that length of stay was inversely associated with success in treatment, i.e., the shorter the length of stay, the greater likelihood of positive clinical outcomes. Boysville research and program staff questioned this assumption.

In addition, Boysville researchers were concerned about the confounding effects of MDSS's inclusion of immediate program failures (i.e., youths who are discharged to another agency very early in their placements) in their computation of average length of stay. Without taking into account the type of release, the inclusion of these youths in the state's statistical computations lowered the average length of stay in agencies with high numbers of early program failures and treated these as successes.

Since BOMIS routinely collects extensive follow-up data on Boysville's former residents, research staff recognized that program effectiveness could not be fully assessed without taking into account the client's discharge status. In response to MDSS's failure to consider client discharge status when studying client post-release status, both executive and research staff at Boysville agreed that performance standards based on this study could have a negative impact on how clients would fare after they returned to their communities.

Ultimately, Boysville executive, research, and program staff alike were critical of MDSS's simplistic approach to arriving at a statistical norm and a performance standard for length of stay by taking the midpoint between the two peaks in their data. Executive staff were critical because, in computing the norm, MDSS policy researchers had lumped together agencies that cared for less seriously troubled youngsters with relatively short-term treatment with agencies such as Boysville that accepted seriously disturbed, multi-problem youths who required long-term treatment. Boysville research staff were critical of the arrival at a statistical norm that did not adequately take into account discharge and post-release status. Lastly, Boysville program staff were critical because of their concern that if the norm were to be applied by MDSS, pressures would be exerted upon them by Boysville administration to release clients who were not ready to be released.

This external policy threat to the future functioning of the agency and other residential child care agencies in the state, and the potential negative impact of the policy on children in care, called for a new study to be conducted with BOMIS data.

THE BOYSVILLE LENGTH OF STAY STUDY

For all of the foregoing reasons, Boysville's Research Department undertook a length of stay study of its own based upon data that are routinely collected by BOMIS. In the study, the BOMIS data base was used, containing information about 583 clients released from Boysville over a three-year period. Included in this population were clients released from Boysville between 1982 and 1984. Unlike the study conducted by MDSS, the Boysville study considered the relationship between post-release status, length of stay, and information on type of release.

Operational Definitions of Success and Failure Post-Termination

The BOMIS study employed the state's operational definition of positive program outcomes as clients who were living in less restrictive settings three months after they were released from Boysville. A less restrictive setting would be their own or a relative's home, a shelter facility, independent living, the Armed Services, or a foster family home.

A negative program outcome was indicated by clients who were in detention centers, jails, secure campus-based programs, private agency programs, or community-based group homes at three-month post-terminations. Thus, a negative outcome was indicated if post-release clients were in settings of equal or more restrictiveness compared to their Boysville placement. Clients who were in more restrictive settings three months after termination were considered "recidivists."

Operational Definition of Success and Failure at Discharge

In contrast to the MDSS study, which offered no data on client discharge status, the BOMIS study based its conception of success and failure at time of discharge on whether client termination was planned or unplanned, respectively. Planned terminations include those who are judged to have received maximum benefits in the program, as well as those who have achieved treatment objectives to the extent deemed realistically possible by Boysville treatment staff. All other types of termination, e.g., truancy, court termination, state termination, parents' removal, or unmanageable behavior were considered unplanned and therefore, failures at discharge.

For the most part, operational definitions employed in the Boysville study were consistent with those used in the 1982 MDSS study and in state policy guidelines. This permitted comparisons of the findings of the two studies and minimized confusion in considering policy implications of the two studies.

As indicated earlier, from the start, Boysville research staff believed that length of stay was not causally tied to success or failure in the way that MDSS assumed. Instead of length of stay determining client outcome, Boysville staff believed that successful or failing "client careers" determined length of stay. Simply stated, failures tended to leave programs earlier than successes because unplanned terminations took place earlier than planned terminations.

Because of this, it was felt that length of stay was not a true predictor of either success upon program completion or post-termination. On the contrary, the three variables, client length of stay, success at termination, and post-termination success, were interconnected in a manner much more complex than suggested in the MDSS study. These complex interrelationships and their policy implications could be properly understood only by the conduct of a multi-variate analysis, taking into account client success or failure at time of termination and after release from the program.

The BOMIS study sought to unravel these relationships and propose sound policies based upon them. More specifically, the Boysville study hypothesized that:

1. There would be a statistically significant positive association between length of stay and successful program outcomes at three months post-termination;
2. There would be a statistically significant positive relationship between length of stay and success at the time of discharge and this

relationship would be stronger than the relationship between length of stay and program outcome at three months post-termination;
3. When type of client discharge is controlled, the relationship between length of stay and client outcome at three months post-termination would be markedly reduced.

BOMIS STUDY FINDINGS

Beginning with the basic length of stay data in the Boysville sample, it was found that the mean length of stay was 11.9 months, the median was 12.2 months, and the mode was 11.7 with a minimum stay of 1.0 month and a maximum stay of 32.7 months.

Study of client background characteristics revealed that the mean age of clients at intake was 15.7 years, with a median age of 15.8 and a modal age of 15.9 years. The youngest client at intake was 12.5 years old, and the oldest was 18.6 years old. Looking at their records with juvenile courts, it was found that the mean, median, and modal number of adjudications was 2, with the minimum 1 and the maximum 22. The mean and median number of previous placements was 1, with the minimum being 0 and the maximum 18. The modal number of previous placements was 0.

Looking at program outcome data, it was found that 55% of Boysville discharges were planned and 45% unplanned. Upon leaving Boysville, 56% of the clients went to less restrictive settings, 18% went to more or equally restrictive settings, and the post-release destinations of 26% of the clients were unknown most often because of truancy. At three months post-placement, 77% of those Boysville clients who could be located were in less restrictive settings and 23% were in more or equally restrictive settings.

Turning to the BOMIS study hypotheses, analysis of the relationship between positive client outcomes at three months after termination and length of stay (see Table 1), indicates, as predicted, a statistically significant, positive association (Tau-C = .24, p < .01). Thus, only 53% of the clients who had been in care between one and six months were in a less restrictive setting three months after release, as compared with more than 85% of the clients who had been in care over 11 months. In contradistinction to the state's assumption, this suggests that the *longer* clients are in care, the *greater* the likelihood they will be in less restrictive settings after they leave the agency.

The next hypothesis tested concerned the relationship between length of stay and type of discharge from the program. As indicated earlier, the

Table 1

Relationship between Positive Client Outcomes at

Three Months after Termination and Length of Stay

Length of Stay in Months

Client Placement 3 Months After Termination	1-5.99	6-10.99	11-12.99	13 & Above	Total
Less Restrictive	53%	70%	86%	85%	77%
More Restrictive	47%	30%	15%	15%	23%
N	72	96	55	231	454

Chi-Square=37.68, df=3, p<.01

Kendall's Tau C=.24

BOMIS study predicted a positive relationship between length of stay and successful discharge. Testing this hypothesis (see Table 2), the BOMIS study found, as predicted, a statistically significant positive relationship between successful termination and length of stay (Tau-C = .58, p < .01). In other words, the longer the length of stay, the more likely the client would be judged a success when he exited the program. Thus, only 15% of the youth in care between one and six months at Boysville received a successful discharge compared to 80% of those in care over 13 months.

Table 3 shows the close relationship between success at program termination and success at three months after release from the agency (Tau-B = .92, p < .001). Thus, 91% of Boysville clients who were successfully discharged from the program were in a less restrictive setting at three months post-release compared to only 55% who were discharged as program failures. These findings lend confidence in the validity and reliability of the BOMIS data-base as well as in the judgment of Boysville treatment staff who determine success upon termination.

Finally, the BOMIS study hypothesized that the relationship between length of stay and client outcome at three months was contingent on the type of discharge. To test this hypothesis, Tables 4 and 5 present the crosstabulations of client outcome at three months after termination, by length of stay, controlling for discharge success or failure, respectively. These crosstabulations, as predicted, clearly show that when one takes into account the type of discharge, length of stay no longer has a statistically significant relationship to post-release client outcome.

Thus, Table 4 indicates that of the successful discharges, 87% of those who were in the program between one and six months are in a less restrictive setting, as compared with 91% of those whose length of stay in the program was 13 months or more.

For program failures, on the other hand, Table 5 reveals a relatively weak, statistically insignificant positive relationship between length of stay and success at three months post-termination (Tau-C = .17, p < .11). Thus, 44% of the program failures who were at Boysville between one and six months were in less restrictive settings post-release as compared with 61% who were in the Boysville program 13 months or more. This also suggested that with program failures, longer lengths of stay had a positive effect, post-discharge.

From these complex findings, the BOMIS study derived a new explanation for the curvilinear relationship found between length of stay and program outcome in the original MDSS study. By failing to take into account the effects of success or failure at discharge on length of stay, and

Table 2

Relationship between Length of Stay
and Discharge Status

Length of Stay in Months

Closing Status	1-5.99	6-10.99	11-12.99	13 & Above	Total
Success	15%	36%	65%	80%	55%
Failure	85%	64%	35%	19%	45%
Totals	130	118	65	270	583

Chi-Square=184.26, df=3, p<.01

Kendall's Tau C=.58

Table 3

Relationship between Discharge Status and Client Status

Three Months after Release from Program

Closing Status

		Success	Failure	Totals
Client placement 3 months after termination	Less Restrictive	91%	55%	77%
	More Restrictive	9%	45%	23%
	Totals	276	178	454

Chi-square=76.38, df=1, p<.001

Kendall's Tau B=.92

Table 4

Relationship between Length of Stay and Client Outcome

Controlling for Success at Time of Termination

Length of Stay in Months

Client placement 3 months after termination		1-5.99	6-10.99	11-12.99	13 & above	Total
	Less Restrictive	87%	92%	92%	91%	91%
	More Restrictive	13%	8%	8%	9%	9%
Totals		15	37	36	188	276

Chi-Square=.40, df=3, p=.94

Kendall's Tau C=.00

Table 5

Relationship between Length of Stay and Client Outcome

at Three Months after Termination Controlling for

Failure at Time of Termination

Length of Stay in Months

Client placement 3 months after termination		1-5.99	6-10.99	11-12.99	13 & above	Total
	Less Restrictive	44%	56%	74%	61%	55%
	More Restrictive	56%	44%	26%	40%	45%
Totals		57	59	19	43	178

Chi-Square=6.08, df=3, p.=.11

Kendall's Tau C=.17

by including in its sample both long- and short-term treatment agencies, Boysville researchers argued that the MDSS study created a spurious two-peaked frequency distribution. Naturally, then, the policy implications drawn from the MDSS study were empirically incorrect, theoretically flawed, and programmatically counterproductive.

POLICY IMPLICATIONS OF THE BOMIS STUDY

The BOMIS study also raised serious questions about whether, as a cost containment approach, a policy dedicated to reduction of length of stay would improve program outcomes and save taxpayers money. By combining short- and long-term treatment programs in their analysis, MDSS arrived at inappropriately low length of stay performance standards for agencies doing long-term treatment. Ironically, in so doing, the MDSS contract also proposed length of stay norms too high for short-term treatment agencies.

The BOMIS study also uncovered potential long-term costs of a short-sighted, cost-containment program to reduce length of stay. By failing to consider the consequences of all program failures that would inevitably result from pressures to reduce length of stay, the proposed MDSS policy did not consider costs to itself of future placements for recidivists. Nor did it take into account costs to society of these placements and the deviant behavior that occasioned them.

Though it is easy to understand why state policymakers would be attracted to measures that would reduce length of stay, their consideration of these measures was too narrowly conceived. Calculating service costs based upon a client's stay at one agency and not on what services cost for the entire placement career of a client who may receive multiple placements leads to poor cost-containment policy (efficiency) as well as to poor program outcomes (effectiveness).

The MDSS approach was not only short-sighted but carried with it the danger of what Etzioni (1964) refers to as goal displacement through over-measurement. In these instances, the performance norm becomes an end in itself rather than a means to true cost-containment or program innovation.

Although these norms were originally developed as a device to reduce placement costs, length of stay norms could easily become a false criterion for MDSSs in judging agencies as effective or ineffective; the former being those with the shortest average length of stay. Failure to factor in the quality of program, characteristics of clients, or program outcomes (at termination and post-release), would create an additional policy problem rather than a solution to a problem. Ironically, if implemented, the unanticipated consequence of the proposed policy to reduce costs was likely to be an increase in the long-term costs of residential child care in the state.

EXTERNAL POLICY ADVOCACY

Once completed, a research report based upon the foregoing analysis was presented to the Assistant Executive Director of Boysville whose agency responsibilities included public policy advocacy. On his recommendation, the report was then presented at a specially organized retreat of executive directors of private child care agencies in Michigan.

Following the retreat, the private agency executives presented the report and its findings to the Governor, State Legislators, the Director of the Department of Social Services, and policy staff from the Office of Children and Youth Services.

Based upon the BOMIS study and support it generated from private child care agencies throughout the state, the 1986 contract language regarding length of stay of clients in residential child care was changed. Agencies would not be held, as originally proposed, to prescribed client lengths of stay for services. Moreover, partly as a result of this experience, Boysville research, policy, and planning staff have since worked more closely with MDSS personnel to find appropriate alternatives for containing costs in residential care. These include the development of In-Home Care, Specialized Foster Care, and Intensive After-Care programs.

REFERENCES

Cartwright, P. (1982). Children's residential services in Michigan: A study of outcomes and costs. Unpublished.

Etzioni, A. (1964). *Modern organizations.* Englewood Cliffs, N.J.: Prentice-Hall, Inc.

Patti, R. (1983). *Social welfare administration.* Englewood Cliffs, N.J.: Prentice-Hall, Inc.

SECTION THREE

Client Characteristics, Family Contacts, and Treatment Outcomes

Sue Ann Savas
Irwin Epstein
Anthony J. Grasso

ABSTRACT. Although other residential treatment agencies are beginning to document successful treatment outcomes, few have attempted to describe a successful residential client profile or the treatment interventions associated with it. Utilizing BOMIS data, this paper identifies some client characteristics and family treatment intervention patterns that are associated with successful program completion at Boysville. The findings emphasize the importance of face-to-face contacts with family members and raise questions about the value of treatment-oriented telephone contacts.

In a time of economic scarcity, funding sources, child welfare advocates, program administrators, and direct service practitioners alike want

Sue Ann Savas is affiliated with Boysville of Michigan, 8744 Clinton-Macon Road, Clinton, MI 49236. Irwin Epstein is affiliated with the School of Social Work, Hunter College, City University of New York, 129 East 79th Street, New York, NY 10021. Anthony Grasso is Director, School of Social Work, University of Nevada at Las Vegas, 4505 Maryland Parkway, Las Vegas, NV 89154-5032.

[Haworth co-indexing entry note]: "Client Characteristics, Family Contacts, and Treatment Outcomes." Savas, Sue Ann, Irwin Epstein, and Anthony J. Grasso. Co-published simultaneously in *Child & Youth Services*, (The Haworth Press, Inc.) Vol. 16, No. 1, 1993, pp. 125-137; and: *Information Systems in Child, Youth, and Family Agencies: Planning, Implementation, and Service Enhancement* (ed: Anthony J. Grasso, and Irwin Epstein) The Haworth Press, Inc., 1993, pp. 125-137. Multiple copies of this article/chapter may be purchased from The Haworth Document Delivery Center. Call 1-800-3-HAWORTH (1-800-342-9678) between 9:00 - 5:00 (EST) and ask for DOCUMENT DELIVERY CENTER.

125

to know what factors are associated with positive client outcomes. As a result, increasing attention has been directed towards the effectiveness and efficiency of residential programs serving adolescent youth (Grasso, Epstein, & Tripodi, 1988; Shennum & Thomas, 1987). With the advent of computerized information systems such as BOMIS, ongoing evaluation of the success of Boysville's child and adolescent treatment programs has become a real possibility (Grasso & Epstein, 1987).

Although other agencies are beginning to document post-placement success, few have attempted to describe a successful residential client profile (Shennum & Thomas, 1987) or the organizational determinants of client success. Which types of clients are more likely to successfully complete a residential program? Do these youths tend to be younger or older, white or minority, from single-parent or two-parent families? And what kinds of staff interventions are associated with successful client outcomes?

PURPOSE OF THE STUDY

Utilizing BOMIS data, this study seeks to identify client characteristics and intervention patterns that are associated with successful program completion. More specifically, the authors were interested in answering the following questions: At the time of discharge, what proportion of clients completed the residential treatment program successfully? Are the clients who successfully completed the treatment program different from those who did not? Are successful client outcomes associated with greater family contact with the program? And does the type of family contact make a difference?

Potential predictors of successful program completion include: (1) the clients' age, race, and number of prior felonious offenses; and 2) the frequency and type of contacts between the worker and the client's family.

BOMIS routinely collects information about a large number of demographic characteristics of children in care at Boysville. In an earlier, unpublished study employing BOMIS data, Whittaker, Overstreet, Grasso, Tripodi, and Boylan (1987) looked at the relationship between client characteristics and treatment patterns at Boysville over the course of a single year. For the purposes of this study, the authors chose to look at the associations between client characteristics and treatment outcomes over the course of five years. In so doing, we focused on those client characteristics found to be associated with successful program outcomes in previous studies. These were age, race, and the number of felonies committed prior to placement.

In two of the previous published studies, age was positively related to successful program outcome (Cowden & Monson, 1969; Shennum & Thomas, 1987). In another, race and prior offenses were also linked to successful completion of the program (Gilliland-Mallo & Judd, 1986). In the latter study, white clients and those clients who were not on probation were more likely to complete the residential program successfully.

After considering the effects of the foregoing client characteristics, this study will explore the relationship between frequency and type of family treatment contact while a youngster is in placement and successful program completion. Family treatment involvement was studied in particular because Boysville is committed to a family-centered approach to service delivery. Thus, intensive family therapy, based on the structural model (Minuchin, 1974) is an integral part of Boysville's treatment program.

Boysville's major commitment to the involvement of parents and other family members began in 1984. At this time, several family treatment workers were hired and trained to work with youths in placement and their families towards the completion of a family-based treatment plan. This programmatic approach was intended to improve family functioning and increase the family's competence thereby avoiding returning the client to an out-of-home placement. For this purpose, a Family Retreat Center was constructed at Boysville's main campus to aid in the treatment process by providing housing for families attending on-campus family treatment sessions. In addition, family treatment workers engage in home visits and telephone contacts with the family members of clients.

A previous study of the linkage between family involvement and client outcome at another agency provided the authors with an external reason for including family contact variables in this study. There, Finkelstein (1974) found that greater parental involvement resulted in shorter lengths of stay for children in residential care.

METHODOLOGY

Profile of the Study Population

This study population is comprised of 608 males who were between the ages of 12 and 18 at the time they were admitted to the program. The average age is 15.5 years. Those studied were residents of Boysville's Clinton Campus who were released from the program between January 1, 1984, and December 31, 1988. Length of stay ranged from one month to 28 months. The average length of stay was 12.4 months. Sixty-three percent of the study population were from single parent families. Forty-eight percent were white, 47% black, and 3% Hispanic.

Only 13% of the population had no documented history of prior legal offenses. Fifty percent of the clients had one or two felonious adjudications prior to placement. Almost 37% of the population had three or more felonies on their court record.

Data Sources

The database for this study is drawn from information that is routinely gathered on three BOMIS forms: The Intake Data Sheet, The Family Service Contact Form, and The Residential Departure Data Sheet.

The Intake Data Sheet, completed by Boysville's Director of Orientation, records the client's age, race, and the number and type of felonious offenses in addition to other background factors and clinical assessment information concerning the client and his family.

The Family Service Contact Form is completed by family workers following each contact of twenty minutes or more (so as to exclude routine contacts) with at least one family member. The information gathered on this instrument includes type of contact (face-to-face or phone), duration of the contact in minutes, and a listing of individuals involved in the contact.

The Residential Departure Data Sheet is completed by the Treatment Coordinator at the time the client is released from the program. This form indicates the client's program completion status as determined by the Treatment Team, the client's placement destination, school placement, grade level, and employment status at release from the program. Because this information as well as information from the other forms are all entered into one, fully integrated, agency-based information system, all data were readily available for analysis despite their different sources.

Measures

The independent variables chosen for this study include the client's age, race, and the number of prior felonious offenses, total number of family contacts, number of face-to-face family contacts and the number of phone family contacts per month in the program.

The client's completion of the program was chosen as the dependent measure. BOMIS records three levels of completion: Boysville Release, Administrative Release, and Program Failure. In this study, Boysville Releases were considered "Successes" in that they refer to those clients who are judged to have successfully achieved all of their treatment objectives by their group treatment peers as well as the staff treatment team.

Those youngsters who received Administrative Releases were categorized as "Moderate Successes" in that they are clients who have completed some, but not all, of their treatment objectives. Nonetheless, they were discharged from placement because the treatment team and youth group felt they had made sufficient gains in treatment to achieve post-placement success.

Those labelled "Program Failures" included: (1) clients who truanted for longer than five days and were dropped from the program; (2) clients with excessive behavior problems where the treatment team determined the client would not be able to earn a successful release; and (3) clients withdrawn from the program by court or state authorities.

FINDINGS

Descriptive analysis of the outcome measure revealed that, of the 608 clients studied, 268 (44%) were "Successes," judged by staff and peers to have completed all treatment objectives; 165 (27%) were classified as "Moderate Successes," having achieved some, but not all, treatment objectives; while the remaining 175 clients (29%) were defined as "Program Failures" who did not successfully complete the Boysville program.

Consistent with the studies by Cowden and Monson (1969) and Shennum and Thomas (1987), further analysis of BOMIS data indicated that, at Boysville, age was related to successful program completion (Table 1). Thus, an analysis of variance indicated that age was positively associated

Table 1

Completion of the Program by Age	
	Mean Age
SUCCESS	15.69 years
MODERATE SUCCESS	15.42 years
PROGRAM FAILURE	15.47 years

F=4.635, p=.014   N=608

with successful program completion (F = 4.635, p = .014). The mean age of the clients who successfully completed the treatment program was 15.69 years. The mean age of the clients who completed the treatment program with moderate success was 15.42 years. Finally, the mean age for those who were defined as program failures was 15.47 years. It is important to note that the major difference here is between clients who successfully complete the program and all others (moderate successes and program failures). However, the overall finding is consistent with previous research on age and program completion.

An analysis of the clients' race and the success of their program completion produced findings that contrast with previous research (Gilliland-Mallo & Judd, 1986). Thus, a Chi-square Test for Independence revealed that there was no significant relationship between race and successful program completion (Chi-square = 1.347, df = 2, NS; Table 2).

The association between successful program completion and the number of felony adjudications incurred prior to placement was also found not to be statistically significant. An Analysis of Variance showed little difference between the mean number of felonies for the three groups (F = 1.372, NS). Nonetheless, the pattern of the relationship is suggestive. The clients who were released from the program as failures had, on average, a greater number of recorded felonies than those who completed the program as successes or moderate successes. In contrast with the relationship between age and successful completion, here the major differences are found between program failures and all others (Table 3).

Controlling for length of stay in the program, the total number of family contacts between family worker and at least one family member was associated with successful completion of the program. Significant differences

Table 2

Completion of the Program by Race		
	WHITE	NON-WHITE
SUCCESS	41.8% (123)	46.2% (145)
MODERATE SUCCESS	27.5% (81)	26.8% (84)
PROGRAM FAILURE	30.7% (90)	27.0% (85)
	100.0 (294)	100.0 (314)

Chi Square=1.347, df=2, NS   N=608

Table 3

Completion of the Program and Pre-Placement Felonies	
	Mean Felonies
SUCCESSES	2.34
MODERATE SUCCESSES	2.21
PROGRAM FAILURES	2.55

F=1.372, NS   N=608

were identified with an Analysis of Variance procedure (F = 2.844, p < .05). The mean number of family contacts that the successful clients received per month in the program was greater than that of the moderate successes. The moderate successes received a greater number of family contacts than did those youths unable to complete the treatment program (Table 4).

By differentiating between face-to-face and therapeutically-oriented phone contacts, a more refined understanding of the association between family contacts and successful program completion was achieved. Thus, families of clients who had successfully completed the program were shown to have had a greater number of face-to-face contacts with their family worker than families of clients who were moderately successful or program failures (F = 22.67, p < .00). On the other hand, the relationship between treatment-oriented phone contacts and successful program completion was not significant (F = 1.52, NS; Table 5).

To further explore the possible interaction between face-to-face and phone treatment contacts, a Family Contact Typology was empirically derived. To do this, face and phone contacts were each divided into high and low groups based on the median number of contacts within each dimension. The number and percentage of clients within each of the four combinations of high and low categories which comprised the typology is described in Table 6. Of the four possible combinations, the greatest percentage of clients (31.7%) received relatively low face and phone contacts. On the other hand, the fewest clients (18.8%) received relatively low face and high phone contacts (Table 6).

A Chi-square Test was performed to examine the relationship between combination of face and phone contacts and successful program completion. This analysis revealed a significant association between the categories of family treatment contact typology and program completion (Chi-

Table 4

Completion of the Program and Family Contacts	
	Mean Monthly Contacts
SUCCESS	1.71
MODERATE SUCCESS	1.53
PROGRAM FAILURE	1.38

F=2.855, p<.05   N=608

Table 5

Type of Family Contact and Completion of the Program		
Mean Contacts per Month in the Program		
	Face-to-Face Contacts*	Phone Contacts
SUCCESS	1.29	.41
MODERATE SUCCESS	.97	.56
PROGRAM FAILURE	.86	.52
F	22.67	1.52

*p<.00   N=608

square = 94.76, df = 6, p < .0005). More specifically, Table 7 shows that while the number of face-to-face family contacts clearly has a positive impact on clients' successful completion of the program, the combination of high face/low phone contacts produced the highest client success rate (64.4%). Of the youths whose families received high face/high phone contacts, 52.7% fully achieved their treatment goals. Alternatively, almost 49% of the youths whose families received low face and low phone contacts were program failures. By contrast, about 40% of those with low face/high phone contacts were program failures. Controlling for a youth's length of stay in the program produced essentially the same results.

In addition to examining the family contact typology and its effect on successful completion of the program, a Chi-Square Test was performed on the relationship between type of family contact while in placement and

Table 6

Family Contact Typology		
	Number	Percentage
1. Low Face/Low Phone	193	31.7
2. High Face/Low Phone	132	21.7
3. Low Face/High Phone	114	18.8
4. High Face/High Phone	169	27.8

N=608

Table 7

Family Contact Typology and Completion of the Program			
	LOW FACE/ LOW PHONE	HIGH FACE/ LOW PHONE	LOW FACE/ HIGH PHONE	HIGH FACE/ HIGH PHONE
	193	132	114	169
SUCCESS	30.1	64.4	31.6	52.7
MODERATE SUCC.	21.2	25.0	28.9	34.3
PROG. FAILURE	48.7	10.6	39.5	13.0

Chi Square=94.77, df=6, p<.0005   N=608

clients' living situations at 12 months post-release. Of the 608 clients in this original study population, BOMIS had 12-month follow-up information on 400. The analysis revealed that type of family contact received was significantly associated with restrictiveness of the client's living situation 12 months after release (Chi-Square = 12.48, df = 3, p = .0059). Thus, over 80% of the former Boysville clients who had received high face/high phone contacts were living in situations that were less restrictive than Boysville (e.g., family home, relatives, extended family) 12 months after discharge. Seventy-seven percent of the former clients who had received high face/low phone contacts were living in less restrictive settings. Alternatively, almost

40% of the clients receiving low face/low phone or low face/high phone were living in more restrictive settings (i.e., jail, detention center, youth home). This additional analysis further supports the treatment efficacy of face-to-face contacts with client family members (Table 8).

Finally, a step-wise multiple regression analysis was conducted to determine amount of variance in successful program completion that was explained by the client's age, and type of family contacts received (see Table 9). This analysis revealed that 9.8% of the variance in program

Table 8

Family Contact Typology and Setting at 12 Months After Release				
	LOW FACE/ LOW PHONE	HIGH FACE/ LOW PHONE	LOW FACE/ HIGH PHONE	HIGH FACE/ HIGH PHONE
	126	92	73	109
LESS RESTRICT.	63.4%	77.2%	63.0%	80.8%
MORE RESTRICT.	36.6%	22.8%	37.0%	19.2%

Chi Square=12.48, df=3, p=.0059   N=400

Table 9

STEP-WISE MULTIPLE REGRESSION ON PROGRAM COMPLETION					
Independent Variables	Step	Multiple R	R Squared	F	Sig. F
Face Contacts	1	.2561	.0658	42.51	p<.0005
Phone Contacts	2	.2936	.0862	28.39	p<.0005
Age	3	.3128	.0978	21.72	p<.0005

N=608

completion was explained by face contacts, phone contacts, and age of the client. Face-to-face contacts was the most powerful predictor, explaining 6.6% of the variance (F = 42.51, p < .0005). Phone contacts explained an additional 2% of the variance (F = 28.39, p < .0005). Age explained 1% of the variance in the clients' completion of the treatment program.

DISCUSSION

The findings from this study indicate there is no significant association between Boysville clients' race or number of prior felonies and their successful completion of Boysville's treatment program. However, there was some indication that number of previous felonies was associated with program failure. More clearly, older clients had a significantly greater degree of success in achieving treatment goals than did younger clients. These findings, though not all significant, demonstrate the need for further inquiry into the effects of clients' background characteristics on their ability to benefit from a residential program such as the one Boysville provides.

A review of recent literature on this topic reveals there have been very few large scale studies of this nature conducted at residential facilities. The results of this study suggest that generalizations about the treatment implications of client background characteristics such as age, race, and prior felonies should be viewed with caution and considered within the context of specific programs.

If, indeed, certain background characteristics are linked to successful program completion, the implications for referring and placing youth into different treatment programs are far-reaching. In addition, program developers, clinical supervisors and program managers would be forced to reexamine their programs to identify which treatment approaches and interventions were more effective with one group of clients compared to another. For instance, older clients were significantly more successful in achieving treatment goals at Boysville. One possible explanation for this might be that the treatment modality offered, although oriented towards here-and-now behaviors, does, in reality, lend itself to insight and introspection. It could be hypothesized that younger clients may not be able to gain as much from this particular treatment approach because of developmental differences between them and older ones. Naturally, this possible explanation should be treated as a set of hypotheses requiring further empirical testing and validation before it is accepted and acted upon.

The analysis of family contact variables provided some insight into the most effective type of family work contacts. The findings suggest that face-to-face contacts are most powerfully linked to a client's successful completion of the program. Although the combination of high face/low phone contacts produced the highest success in achieving treatment goals at discharge, high face/high phone was highest in predicting a less restrictive living situation at 12 months post-discharge.

We can speculate about why high face/low phone might be associated with more successful completion of treatment goals than high face/high phone or other family contact configurations. Among those receiving high face contacts and doing well, therapeutically-oriented phone contacts may be considered less significant and may be less likely to occur. Those with high face and high phone contacts may be different kinds of cases in which phone contacts are used to support less effective face-to-face sessions. Alternatively, phone contacts may contribute to the effectiveness of treatment when face-to-face contacts are low. These considerations await further empirical investigation. What our findings do suggest is that face-to-face treatment contacts are quite effective, but the impact of the treatment-oriented phone contacts on the treatment process is at this point ambiguous.

Future studies should be directed as well toward identifying other factors that may determine the types of contacts a family receives. Perhaps family workers conducting a greater number of phone contacts rather than face contacts believe that phone contacts are an effective substitute for face-to-face contacts. Or, workers reluctant to make visits to homes in unsafe neighborhoods may substitute phone contacts in their place. The amount of work time lost while traveling to the family session may lead workers to opt for phone contacts. "Down time" is clearly greater with face-to-face contacts compared to phone contacts.

Another interpretation for the discrepancy in the types of contacts delivered by workers involves resistant families. These families may refuse face-to-face contacts but accept treatment services over the phone. Maybe family workers are conducting face-to-face contacts with those families who are more "attractive" and have a greater chance for success, even before the treatment process begins. Some workers have even suggested that phone contacts are underreported because the workers do not have time to accurately document phone contacts.

All of the foregoing possibilities call for further exploration. Whatever these explorations uncover, the knowledge that face-to-face contacts are a statistically significant predictor of successful attainment of treatment goals has important implications for future resource allocation and improved service delivery at Boysville.

REFERENCES

Cowden, J. E., & Monson, L. (1969). An analysis of some relationships between personality adjustment, placement, and post-release adjustment of delinquent boys. *Journal of Research in Crime and Delinquency, 6,* 63-70.

Finkelstein, N. E. (1974). Family participation in residential treatment. *Child Welfare, 53,* 570-576.

Gilliland-Mallo, D., & Judd, P. (1986). The effectiveness of residential care facilities for adolescent boys. *Adolescence, 21,* 310-321.

Grasso, A., & Epstein, I. (1987). Management by measurement: Organizational dilemmas and opportunities. *Administration in Social Work, 11,* 89-100.

Grasso, A., Epstein, I., & Tripodi, T. (1988). Agency-based research utilization in a residential childcare agency. *Administration in Social Work, 12,* 61-80.

Minuchin, S. (1974). *Families and family therapy.* Cambridge, MA: Harvard University Press.

Shennum, W., & Thomas, C. (1987). A computer-based system for processing client behavior data in a residential treatment program. *Residential Treatment for Children & Youth, 5,* 83-93.

Whittaker, J., Overstreet, E. J., Grasso, A., Tripodi, T., & Boylan, F. (1987). Multiple indicators of success in residential youth care and treatment. *American Journal of Orthopsychiatry, 58,* 143-147.

Youth and Family Characteristics, Treatment Histories, and Service Outcomes: Some Preliminary Findings from the Boysville Research Program

James K. Whittaker
Tony Tripodi
Anthony J. Grasso

ABSTRACT. Based upon BOMIS data, this paper explores youth and family characteristics and treatment processes associated with successful client outcomes at Boysville. Although the study is descriptive rather than predictive, it offers several implications for practice. It also demonstrates the basic research potential of BOMIS data.

James K. Whittaker is affiliated with the School of Social Work, University of Washington, 4101 Fifteenth Avenue N.W., JH-30, Seattle, WA 98185. Tony Tripodi is affiliated with the School of Public Affairs and Services, North Miami Campus, Florida International University, North Miami, FL 33181. Anthony J. Grasso is Director, School of Social Work, University of Nevada at Las Vegas, 4505 Maryland Parkway, Las Vegas, NV 89154-5032.

[Haworth co-indexing entry note]: "Youth and Family Characteristics, Treatment Histories, and Service Outcomes: Some Preliminary Findings from the Boysville Research Program." Whittaker, James K., Tony Tripodi, and Anthony J. Grasso. Co-published simultaneously in *Child & Youth Services*, (The Haworth Press, Inc.) Vol. 16, No. 1, 1993, pp. 139-153; and: *Information Systems in Child, Youth, and Family Agencies: Planning, Implementation, and Service Enhancement* (ed: Anthony J. Grasso, and Irwin Epstein) The Haworth Press, Inc., 1993, pp. 139-153. Multiple copies of this article/chapter may be purchased from The Haworth Document Delivery Center. Call 1-800-3-HAWORTH (1-800-342-9678) between 9:00 - 5:00 (EST) and ask for DOCUMENT DELIVERY CENTER.

139

A sign over the portal of the famed Tavistock clinic in London succinctly summarizes the proper relationship of research and practice in a clinical setting: *No research without service.* Boysville of Michigan is committed to a similar philosophy. The short- and long-term purposes of research are to inform, enhance, and, ultimately, improve the professional help offered to troubled youths and their families. This is the core of Boysville's mission, and all of its numerous research activities are so directed: mission-oriented research *is* the research program. What the philosopher Santayana described as "impassioned empiricism" informs and inspires all phases of the research process. What this means, in a practical sense, is that researchers and clinical staff begin and end with the question(s): How will this study improve the lives of youths in care? Of their families? What potential implications will there be for practice? Relevance for practice and methodological rigor are constantly weighed against each other, though the strongly felt bias is that one *need not* be substituted for the other.

The purpose of the exploratory study reported here was to shed light on factors affecting "successful treatment" (defined here as planful discharge from Boysville) and subsequent community adaptation. What factors differentiate those who succeed or fail in the Boysville program, and what implications do these differences hold for improving practice with individual youths and their families? Since the primary outcome of interest was nominal–success/failure–most results are expressed as mean differences between these groups. Relationships are intended to be descriptive rather than predictive or causal. This particular investigation is best viewed in the context of the total Boysville research effort as reported in this volume.

THE STUDY SAMPLE

The population in this analysis consisted of 239 youths released from the campus-based program, Clinton, Michigan, in 1984 and 1985. Youths who received either a successful (planned) or an unsuccessful (unplanned) termination and who were in the program for more than 30 days were used as part of the analysis. The campus population was chosen because this part of the agency received the greatest impact of the research project and provided the most reliable information in the present Boysville system. Since we wished to look at relationships between black and white children, and since the population of other minority children was less than 1%, the others were eliminated from this study.

Characteristics of youths at intake (see Table 1) were as follows: *age*

Table 1   Youth Characteristics at Intake 1984-85 (n=239)

Variable	Mean (st. dev.)	Percent
Age	15.50 (1.03)	
Race		
White		52.7%
Black		47.3
Placement Type		
Delinquent		51.0%
Dependent-neglect		49.0
Prior living situation		
Youth home		50.6%
Home		30.1
Shelter		11.3
Private facility		3.3
Other		4.7
Physical or sexual abuse		
Yes		15.5%
No		23.8
Not determined		60.7
Prior adjudications	1.80 (0.79)	

(mean, 15.53; range, 12.26 to 17.49); *race* (white, 52.7%; black, 47.3%); *type of placement* (delinquent, 51%; dependent-neglect 49%); *type of referral* (Juvenile Court, 3.3%; CAR, 33.9%; DSS-CCRA, 28.5%; DSS-other, 33.9%; public mental health facility, 3.3%; group home; 1.7%; other, 3%). Information on physical and/or sexual abuse was sketchy: 15.5% of the youths were reported by workers as having been abused, while nearly 24% were assessed to have not been subject to abuse. For over 60% of the cases, the fact of abuse could neither be confirmed nor rejected. The mean number of previous placements was 0.99.

Salient family factors are presented in Table 2. Nearly 80% of families expressed a willingness to participate in family treatment, less than 2% declined, and the responses of the remaining parents were unknown. More than half of the boys (63.5%) came from single-parent households (divorced, 32.0%; separated, 9.3%; widowed, 9.3%; unmarried, 12.9%), and approximately one-third (36.4%) came from two-parent families. Family contact was measured in a variety of ways. Means and ranges for contacts were: *Meeting length* (minutes) (73.42; 20.00 to 164.00); *phone contacts* (7.74; 0 to 123.00); *total face-to-face contacts* (10.27; 0 to 55.00); *overall*

Table 2   Family Characteristics at Intake 1984-85 (n=239)

Variable	Percent
Type of household	
Nuclear*	15.9%
Single parent**	69.9
Extended***	9.2
Adoptive	4.2
Other	0.8
Parent willingness to participate in tx	
Yes	77.8%
No	1.7
Not determined	20.5

* includes families with two biological parents or two parent reconstituted households (1 biological parent)

** limited to child's family having one biological parent

*** one or two adult relatives as head(s) of household

total family contacts (18.02; 0 to 169.00); and *total* minutes of family *work* (881.04; 20.00 to 4,015.00). The average length of stay for Boysville youths was 12.5 months.

METHODOLOGY

Data were obtained for all youths discharged from the Boysville campus program in 1984 and 1985 (N = 239). In some instances, sample size will reflect less than 239 due to incomplete data on all measures for all youths. Cases were categorized as "success"/"nonsuccess" and appropriate comparisons performed. In the main, these consisted of T-tests, crosstabs, and, where appropriate, correlational measures. Since this time period parallels the implementation of the Boysville management information and research system, missing data were not uncommon. Gaps in data are reported throughout.

FINDINGS

As noted, the primary outcome measure was the student's release status. Planned or administrative release was defined as success. All other possible release circumstances were viewed as failure. Based on this definition, the Boysville success rate was approximately 70%. A second outcome measured students' adjustment three months after Boysville release. This variable is a calculated score given to clients on a zero to twenty point range that is determined by the living situation of a client, whether or not they are in school or have graduated from school, whether or not they work and how many police contacts they have had since termination. Zero is equal to failure, one to nine is "poor adjustment," 10-15 "satisfactory adjustment," and 16-20 is "excellent adjustment." Finally, results are presented for an additional outcome variable, placement destination at case closing. This measure is closely related to the Boysville treatment success variable, but results vary depending on the outcome used.

RELATIONSHIPS AMONG OUTCOME MEASURES

Among successful cases, 91% (n = 152) were placed in less restrictive settings; 73.3% (n = 28) of the 38 failures were sent to a more restrictive environment. Despite a clear relationship between these variables, success/failure was not synonymous with placement type. Also, as expected, case termination is related to a student's placement setting at three-month follow-up. Among successes, 88.4% (n = 129) were in less restrictive environments; only 36% (n = 18) of failures were comparably placed.

RELATIONSHIPS BETWEEN OUTCOMES, TREATMENT PROCESS VARIABLES, AND INTAKE CHARACTERISTICS

Family/youth treatment process and termination data are presented in Tables 3 and 4. Successful cases, on average, stayed in the program longer (14.1 vs. 8.7 months, $p < .001$), had twice the family-worker face-to-face contact rate (12.1 vs. 6.1, $p < .001$), significantly more minutes of family work by staff (1047 vs. 485 mins., $p < .001$), and higher total family contacts (including telephone) (20.7 vs. 11.8, $p = .002$). These differences occurred despite comparable parental willingness to be involved in the Boysville treatment process. Nearly all parents indicated a willingness to participate in the treatment process (97% of successes; 100% of failures). Conversely, failures had significantly greater involvement with discipline problems as measured by intensive care unit (ICU) usage (2.3 vs. 1.3; $p = .003$) and treatment truancies (2.2 vs. 0.9; $p < .001$).

Table 3   Family Treatment Process and Successful Boysville Termination
1984-85 (n=239)

	Treatment Indicators	Successful Termination X̄	Nonsuccessful Termination X̄
a)	family-worker face-to-face contacts	12.1	6.1**
b)	telephone contacts	8.6	5.7 (ns)
c)	total family contacts	20.7	11.8*
d)	total minutes of family work	1047	485**

  * p_0.01
 ** p_0.001

Table 4   Youth Treatment Process and Successful Boysville Termination
1984-85 (n=239)

	Treatment Indicators	Successful Termination X̄	Nonsuccessful Termination X̄
a)	length of stay	14.1 mos.	8.7*mos.
b)	placement in intensive care usage (ICU)	2.3	1.3*
c)	truancies	2.2	0.9**

Given these results, an interesting question arises: beyond differences in length of stay, what intake differences among adolescents or their families existed which might account for treatment process and outcome findings? Possible explanations might include external constraints, such as distance from Boysville or difficulty scheduling contacts due to parents' work schedules. Interestingly, the two treatment outcome groups did not differ significantly on number of worker telephone contacts with students' families (8.6 vs. 5.7; $p > .05$). A partial answer to this question of initial differences was found in subsequent analyses. First, although successes and failures did not differ in mean age at intake (15.6 vs. 15.5), the latter group had a significantly higher number of adjudications prior to Boysville placement (2.0 vs. 1.7; $p = .03$).

Second, race differences were found on some treatment process measures. Black students had fewer family worker contacts than whites (8.9 vs. 11.5; $p = .03$) and fewer minutes of family work (702 vs. 1031; $p < .001$), although length of stay was comparable for both groups. Interestingly, white youths had a higher adjudication rate prior to entering Boysville (2.0 vs. 1.6; p < .001) and higher truant activity during treatment (1.6 vs. 1.1; p < .015). Yet black students apparently experienced more problems in treatment as reflected in higher usage of the intensive care unit (1.9 vs. 1.3; p < .02). On further discussion with clinical staff, this interpretation proved to be erroneous, as will be explained in the discussion section.

Beyond treatment process-race differences, blacks and whites did not differ in treatment outcome. Approximately 70% of both groups were labelled successes; again, "success" is not a surrogate measure for placement destination–a more sensitive indicator of treatment outcome. Black youths had nearly twice the rate of placement into more restrictive settings after release (26.7% vs. 15.4%; $X2 = 3.33$; p = .07) ("X2" = chi-square). Within three months after leaving Boysville, this gap in placement destination widened. At the three-month follow-up, 33% (n = 32) of blacks were in more restrictive placement as compared to 17% (n = 17) of white youths ($X^2 = 5.72$; p = .02). Thus, however anomalous the relationship between client race and actual treatment, race differences are not reflected in success rates but do appear in the placement data. The empirical basis for this discrepancy has not yet been examined.

A possible explanation for placement differences includes resource availability within urban and suburban environments, since the majority of black youths come from inner city areas. Racial differences in treatment process and intake characteristics also require further work. It is likely that youth, family, and institutional background attributes account for at least some of the differences between whites and blacks. However, such findings may not be sufficient explanations. Future analyses will focus on within-race relationships to characterize more fully the typical client and his/her history both before and during Boysville placement.

Based on the available intake data, another intake measure may be related to treatment and outcomes. A youth's living situation prior to entering Boysville may be associated with exit status. Adolescents placed from youth homes (n = 121) had a relatively high failure rate (n = 47; 38.8%). Interestingly, the other intake living situation with a high failure rate involved students placed from their homes. Twenty of these 72 adolescents (27.8%) were deemed failures at case closing. Again, actual placement destination does not conform completely to the treatment outcome measure. Among youth home cases, 28.2% (n = 29) went to more restrictive settings, whereas only 11.9% (n = 7) of youths who entered Boysville from home ended up in a more restrictive placement at case closing.

These results may do little more than highlight differences between the Boysville definition of success and placement destination. Likewise, if placement destination is itself an important outcome, then these differences could indicate that the measurement of success/failure as the primary outcome of interest should be reexamined. This illustrates the advantages of an ongoing data collection system where it is possible to consider alternative definitions of important but complex concepts such as treatment success.

To summarize thus far, treatment process appears positively related to client outcomes. In addition, some client demographic and intake variables are also related to the treatment process and case closing measures. Because of this, further work is needed to explain initial differences in Boysville youths, and, then, to either control for these differences when examining outcomes or perform outcome analyses separately for each group of interest. It also bears repeating that demographic intake measures may be best understood as proxies for other unanalyzed client or family variables. It makes little sense to say that adolescents from both youth homes and family-of-origin settings are more likely to fail at Boysville than youths from foster homes, shelters, and so on, unless we can further characterize what factors, if any, are common to these various living situations.

PLACEMENT DESTINATION

Approximately 80% of the youths were discharged into less restrictive settings. Comparisons of less and more restrictive placement groups revealed expected differences. Those in less restrictive placements at case closing were Boysville residents longer (13.8 vs. 11.8 mos.; p = .015), had greater family worker contacts (12.2 vs. 7.0; p < .001), more minutes of family work (1053 vs. 589; p < .001), less intensive care unit usage (1.2 vs. 3.0; p < .001), and fewer truancies (1.1 vs. 1.7; p = .025). Nonsignificant differences occurred among intake and treatment process variables. The two groups were of comparable age, had equal numbers of adjudications and statistically equivalent total family and phone contacts. As noted earlier, three-month adjustment scores were much higher for the less restrictive group.

ADDITIONAL RESULTS

Other analyses were performed on subsets of the available cases. For example, comparisons were completed for abused vs. nonabused cases at intake. Sexual and physical abuse cases were analyzed together. Future versions of the intake instrument can yield finer distinctions for this variable. No differences were found between these two groups on racial make-up, treatment process variables (e.g., total worker contacts), success rate (closing status), or placement at termination and three-month follow-up. Differences did occur for one background measure and one process measure. Non-abused cases had, on average, a higher adjudication rate (1.96 vs. 1.51; p = .007). During treatment, abused students had a much higher mean ICU usage (2.59 vs. 0.82; p < .001). These results, though, are limited by incomplete sample coverage. Less than 100 youths had valid codes for the abuse variable. It is unknown how results would appear with a more representative Boysville sample.

Similarly, the sample of 239 boys was divided into two groups according to delinquent status: 122 delinquents and 117 boys with dependent or neglect status. These groups were compared on family contact, family treatment interaction, adolescent coping, and available background variables. Using a criterion of statistical significance at p < .05, there were no differences between delinquents and non-delinquents on family contact, family interaction, and background variables with the exception of living situation at intake (Chi-square = 6.94; p = .008), where a higher proportion of delinquents (66.4%) were in more restrictive settings than non-delinquents (48.7%).

Three other variables for which there were statistically significant differences indicated that boys with dependent-neglect status were more likely to be successful than delinquent boys. While at Boysville, the mean number of times using the intensive care unit was 1.902 for delinquents and 1.239 for non-delinquents (t = 2.37; p < .019); and at discharge from Boysville, dependent-neglected boys were more likely to be judged as successful (76.1%) compared to delinquents (63.9%; Chi-square = 3.62; p < .057). This persisted three months after discharge, when the mean adjustment score for non-delinquents (15.66) was significantly higher (t = 3.13, p < .002) than for delinquents (12.534).

IMPLICATIONS FOR TREATMENT PLANNING AND FUTURE RESEARCH

This preliminary investigation yielded several findings of interest that will help shape the course of future investigation within the Boysville research program, as well as alter the course of selected youth care and family work practices.

Comparability with Other Intake Studies

Our analysis yielded results strikingly similar to a recent large-scale survey of residential treatment agencies conducted in California (Fitzharris, 1985). For example, both studies reveal a disproportionate number of single-parent-headed families (over 50%) beset by multiple problems. The California study identified "inability to control the child" as the most frequently occurring parental difficulty, present in nearly 70% of families. While this factor was not explicitly measured in the present study, anecdotal evidence from clinical staff suggests this may be the case at Boysville as well. The profile of families that emerges is one of disproportionately single parents unable to control the child's behavior; it poses, as we shall see, a challenging task for family work within the agency.

Other points of similarity between the two studies included the finding that youths enter residential treatment through multiple pathways and for differing reasons. For example, in both studies, nearly two-thirds of youths entering residential care from juvenile correction services were entering a *less* restrictive placement. This empirical evidence counters the popular perception that group care is, by definition, an end of the line, "last resort" alternative for children and youths. By contrast, nearly 25% of youths in the present study and a comparable number from the California study entered residential care from their own homes. Future analyses will seek to confirm what proportion of Boysville youths entering directly from their own homes did so because residential placement was the treatment of choice, or because of the unavailability of more preventive, home-based services. Even this present preliminary analysis, however, illustrates the value of routinely collected and monitored intake data for assessment of severity of parent-child problems, pathways into placement, and family constellations. Ultimately, systematic assessment of such routinely gathered data will aid administration in developing assessments of risks, severity, and acuity.

The criterion question. The present study highlights several important issues around the definition of "success" in residential treatment. Boysville's past measure of success–planned termination–proved to be a less valid indicator of outcome than planned termination coupled with placement destination, i.e., to a more or less restrictive environment. Taken together, these two indicators provide a reasonably good measure of how successful Boysville is in providing care, education, and treatment for youths–at least to the point of discharge from the program. More fundamentally, our exploratory study suggests the utility of the Boysville data system of documenting "success" at multiple points in the treatment process: intake, during treatment, at discharge, and post-placement.

As mentioned, Boysville is a "step down" (less restrictive placement) for a significant number of delinquent youths entering care. Boysville's ability to care for and successfully treat such youths in a less restrictive setting should be considered in developing an overall measure of "success." We believe other indicators are present during treatment–decreased violent behavior, for example–and at discharge and post-placement. Work in progress is attempting to delineate the multiple indicators of success in the Boysville program (Whittaker et al., 1987). Again, the presence of the data system makes such analysis possible.

Family involvement. Continuity with the family of origin and family support have been shown to be associated, frequently, with successful community reintegration of youths from residential care and treatment (Whittaker & Pecora, 1984). Conversely, the absence of post-placement support, both from and to the family, has been associated with the decay of residential treatment effects in several studies (Nelson, Singer, & Johnsen, 1978; Lewis, 1982).

We were interested in what factors other than length of stay account for higher participation of families with "successful" youths (i.e., those who planfully terminate), despite an equal willingness to participate in the youth's treatment at the point of intake. One variable on which successful/non-successful youths differed significantly was number of prior adjudications. We speculate that this might suggest that non-success youths were more out of the control of their parents and, thus, the parents were less inclined to participate in the treatment process. Future analysis will attempt to identify patterns of family participation for successful youths, using the multiple indicators that Boysville routinely tracks. These include the following items: face-to-face contacts, telephone contacts, family therapy vs. delivery of concrete services, etc. Ultimately, our goal is to provide a composite measure of family continuity based on intake characteristics of youths and their families which will provide the base for differential treatment planning.

Race differences. Black youths at Boysville are planfully discharged in the same proportion as their white counterparts, though they disproportionately move on to more restrictive settings. Future analysis will seek to confirm to what extent this reflects more severity in acting-out behavior or lack of post-placement resources in the urban environments to which most black youths return. We have reason to question the first explanation, as our data indicate that, at the point of intake, white youths had a significantly higher rate of adjudication than did blacks. For now, the differences in black/white placement destination remain a matter of continuing agency concern.

What appeared at first glance to be black/white differences during treatment–reflected, for example, in higher use by blacks of the intensive care unit for acting-out behavior–were seen, after discussion with clinical staff, as simply reflections of different *patterns* of acting out between black and white youths. Particularly, on the rural campus which comprises the core of the Boysville program, inner city black youths tended to act out on campus more, while their white counterparts tended to run from the program more frequently. In group homes closer to core urban areas, this pattern was reversed. Thus, what appeared at first glance as differences in treatment participation are better explained as a consequence of the ecology of the treatment setting. As reported, in the area of family participation, black families participated less than whites, with one significant exception, despite an equal expressed willingness to participate at the point of intake. Given the weight of evidence previously cited on the importance of family involvement, we were interested in why these differences existed. Discussions with clinical staff revealed a number of specific barriers to family involvement that were particularly problematic for blacks. Many of these were already being addressed by changes in agency policy and practices that occurred subsequent to the collection of our data.

Transportation, for example, proved to be a major impediment to black families, particularly for campus-based activities. Now, agency policy is that transportation should not constitute a barrier to family involvement, and regular van service is provided between the campus and major metropolitan areas served by Boysville. Similarly, a pilot center has been developed in the urban area to provide family services closer to the communities in which youths reside. Training is contemplated around issues of both cultural sensitivity and legitimate safety concerns regarding "fear of the neighborhoods." Finally, this agency has long recognized the under-representation of minority staff in the family work area, and a concerted effort is underway to recruit greater numbers.

In the area of family composition, while the percent of single-parent-headed households was roughly comparable between black and white youths entering Boysville, blacks more routinely reported an extended family network. As reported, blacks had less family contact than whites, except telephone contact, even though length of stay at Boysville was virtually the same for both groups. We speculated that this differential amount of family work coupled with: (1) higher rates of campus acting out by blacks (as reflected in more frequent placement in the intensive care unit); (2) greater numbers of black youths from extended families; and (3) equivalent amounts of telephone contact with black and white families (despite fewer overall family contacts for blacks) suggested a different strategy for work with some black families.

For example, might a more systematic and routine initiation of telephone contact between Boysville staff, youths, and extended family members which emphasized *some* area of positive achievement in the group work program (academic, sports, cottage group participation) serve to reinforce positive behavior on campus while, at the same time, increasing the frequency of total family involvement? Other suggestions under consideration include identification of strategies designed to augment the informal support networks available to black families through the recruitment of additional "natural helpers" (Whittaker & Tracy, 1986).

Finally, the barriers to locating less restrictive post-placement settings for black youths are being examined with an eye toward alternate solutions. Again, the presence of continuously monitored treatment process data on black and white youths and their families allows for a "fine tuning" of existing program components as well as experimentation. In future analyses, we hope to identify what patterns among black and white youth, what family characteristics, and what patterns of family involvement (e.g., telephone, face-to-face, parental-extended family network) lead to more planned terminations to less restrictive post-placement settings. In a general way, future research efforts will explore the following anticipated relationships among variables presently tracked in the management information system with respect to black and white youths and families.

Figure 1 indicates anticipated relationships among the sets of variables previously described. It is expected that family background variables will be related to family treatment interactions, which in turn should be related to family contact, which is hypothesized to be related to success. Correspondingly, adolescent background variables are expected to be related to adolescent coping, which should be related to family interaction and family contact; as previously indicated, length of stay should be directly related to success.

One final finding of interest emerged from our present study. While data on maltreatment prior to coming to Boysville were imcomplete, no differences were found on most treatment process and outcome measures between abused and non-abused youths. However, abused youths did act out more on campus and were more frequent users of the intensive care unit. We want to explore, with clinical staff, what this finding might mean, particularly in terms of a more intense treatment effort for identified abused youths.

In summary, our preliminary analysis of youth and family characteris-

FIGURE 1. A Schematic Relationship Of Sets Of Variables To Success

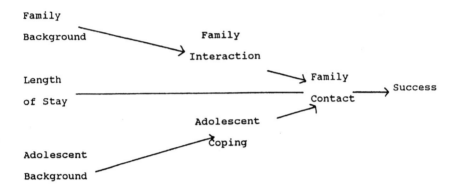

tics, treatment processes, and outcomes yielded several significant findings with implications for future research and practice experimentation. We are genuinely excited at the prospects for using routinely gathered data to inform practice and mission-oriented research with troubled youths and their families.

ACKNOWLEDGEMENT

The authors wish to acknowledge the support and helpful critiques received from Brother Francis Boylan, Edward J. Overstreet, and Brother James Caley at Boysville; our colleagues on the Boysville National Research Advisory Committee: Irwin Epstein (Chair), Hamilton McCubbin, Donnell M. Pappenfort, Dee Morgan Kilpatrick, and Shirley Vining Brown; David Fine of the University of Washington; the Boysville research and clinical staff; and the youths and their families who made this research effort possible.

REFERENCES

Fitzharris, T. L. (1985). *The foster children of California: Profiles of 10,000 children in residential care.* Sacramento: Children's Services Foundation.
Lewis, W. W. (1982). Ecological factors in successful residential treatment. *Behavioral Disorders, 7,* 149-156.

Nelson, R. H., Singer, M. J., & Johnsen, L. O. (1978). The application of a residential treatment evaluation model. *Child Care Quarterly, 7,* 164-175.

Whittaker, J., Overstreet, E. J., Grasso, A., Tripodi, T., & Boylan, F. (1987). Multiple indicators of success in residential youth care and treatment. *American Journal of Orthopsychiatry, 58,* 143-147.

Whittaker, J. K., & Pecora, P. (1984). A research agenda for residential care. In T. Philpot (Ed.), *Group care practice: The challenge of the next decade.* Surrey, U. K.: Business Press International-Community Care, 71-87.

Whittaker, J. K., & Tracy, E. (1986). Supporting families: Linking formal and informal helping in family preservation services. *Permanency Report.* Washington, DC: Child Welfare League of America.

Monitoring Family System Functioning, Family, and Adolescent Coping in the Context of Residential Treatment: Implications for Program Management, Practice Innovation, and Research

Hamilton McCubbin
Stephen A. Kapp
Anne I. Thompson

ABSTRACT. The basic research value of an agency-based information system is a function of its ability to examine and test social science theories, propositions, and hypotheses. This paper employs BOMIS data to test a set of hypotheses regarding the effects of youth coping patterns and family system types on successful program completion and post-release outcomes. The findings have implications for treatment change as well as for family and adolescent development research.

Hamilton McCubbin and Anne I. Thompson are affiliated with the School of Family Resources & Consumer Sciences, University of Wisconsin, 1300 Linden Drive, Madison, WI 53706. Stephen A. Kapp is affiliated with Boysville of Michigan, 8744 Clinton-Macon Road, Clinton, MI 49236.

[Haworth co-indexing entry note]: "Monitoring Family System Functioning, Family, and Adolescent Coping in the Context of Residential Treatment: Implications for Program Management, Practice Innovation, and Research." McCubbin, Hamilton, Stephen A. Kapp, and Anne I. Thompson. Co-published simultaneously in *Child & Youth Services,* (The Haworth Press, Inc.) Vol. 16, No. 1, 1993, pp. 155-173; and: *Information Systems in Child, Youth, and Family Agencies: Planning, Implementation, and Service Enhancement* (ed: Anthony J. Grasso, and Irwin Epstein) The Haworth Press, Inc., 1993, pp. 155-173. Multiple copies of this article/chapter may be purchased from The Haworth Document Delivery Center. Call 1-800-3-HAWORTH (1-800-342-9678) between 9:00 - 5:00 (EST) and ask for DOCUMENT DELIVERY CENTER.

In their extensive discussion of agency-based information systems, Epstein and Grasso (1987) argued for the importance of unique, on-site data systems that can serve as a major source of new knowledge about clients, staff, program, and policy. Unlike other agency-based data systems (Conrad, 1985; Fanshel, 1977), the Boysville Management Information System (BOMIS) was represented as special, described as a fully integrated, computerized, clinically sensitive, and applied research-oriented system, also designed to promote basic research on adolescent development and family functioning.

Ultimately, the value of a database such as BOMIS will be determined, in part, by its ability to offer meaningful information which can be used in a systematic way to examine and test theories, propositions, and hypotheses. The purpose of this investigation is to examine the efficacy of the BOMIS system. Even in its early stages of development and implementation, BOMIS has proven a viable data system for advancing research on the Typology Model of Family Stress, Adjustment, and Adaptation (McCubbin & McCubbin, 1987) and for providing a framework for explaining and understanding young adult behavior in a residential treatment program as well as post-treatment adaptation.

THE INTERACTION OF RESIDENTIAL TREATMENT AND THE MANAGEMENT INFORMATION AND RESEARCH SYSTEM

The relevant information is compiled by BOMIS at three discernible phases of youth involvement in Boysville's residential program (see Figure 1): (1) the baseline and intake phase; (2) the treatment and launching phase; and (3) the adaptation follow-up phase. At the intake phase, information concerning client characteristics such as previous placements in other programs, family type, family functioning, and youth coping as well as race, gender, and prior adjudications, are compiled.

Since Boysville's treatment technology is heavily committed to Structural Family Therapy, BOMIS routinely compiles family system and functioning information based on several standardized measures. With these background and diagnostic data, agency staff are able to systematically assess youths and families and plan a treatment strategy.

BOMIS stores and analyzes information on worker interventions, family involvement, and family contacts, as well as family functioning at the treatment and launching phase. This information is used primarily for modifying and improving treatment interventions, but secondarily for program management decisions. This phase includes a point at which the youth makes the transition from residential care. During this phase, BOMIS compiles information on the conditions of each youth's termination with the program, including data regarding successful completion, placement destination, completion of the family work program, and individual and family coping. This information is used to assess whether individual youths and their families have achieved treatment goals and, through aggregation, makes possible individual worker, unit, and program level evaluation.

Finally, at the follow-up stage, information is compiled at three, twelve, and eighteen months after the youth's launching. These data contain current youth placement destination, that is, whether the youth is placed in the family, jail, or other setting; whether the youth is working or in school; whether or not the youth had other contacts with the police; as well as family and youth coping. This information encourages Boysville to draw conclusions or make predictions about the impact of the program on youth.

THE TYPOLOGY MODEL OF FAMILY
AND YOUTH ADJUSTMENT AND ADAPTATION

The Typology Model of Family Stress, Adjustment, and Adaptation (McCubbin & McCubbin, 1987) incorporated into BOMIS (see Figure 1) is used at Boysville to assess and study family and adolescent interaction and adaptation. It is based on five fundamental assumptions about the interaction of family functioning, youth development, residential treatment, and youth adaptation following treatment. First, families faced with the placement of a member in residential care are confronted with a transitional crisis demanding major changes in the ways the family unit behaves and adapts. The degree of residential care success for both family and youth is dependent upon background characteristics of the family unit and the youth involved. The type of family structure (i.e., single-parent, two-parent, etc.), and ethnicity have a major bearing upon outcome of residential care.

Second, families create for themselves specific and predictable styles of functioning (i.e., balanced, mid-range, and extreme) which can be measured and identified. These patterns have predictive power in explaining which adolescents and young adults are most likely to adapt in residential care and post-residential settings.

Third, families develop basic and unique strengths and capabilities designed to protect the family system from breakdown in crisis situations and to foster the family's adaptation following a major change and transition. These basic strengths include cohesiveness and adaptability; involvement in care; and openness, understanding, and cooperation, as well as coping strategies for dealing with crises. Families may emphasize such coping as reframing and passive appraisal, while youths may underscore such coping responses as ventilation or seeking professional help and assistance. These strengths have great buffering (stress reducing) qualities as well as adaptive (promoting change and stability after change) power.

Fourth, the course and level of success of adaptation for youth involved in residential care will be shaped by interaction of family backgrounds with condition and level of functioning of the family system at time of placement in residential care, and coping repertoires of both parents and youth.

Fifth, the social context, in this case the residential program, particularly with its emphasis on treating the family as a unit, will have a major bearing upon the youth's successful completion of the program and successful adaptation three, six, and 12 months after residential care.

Utilizing BOMIS data and the Family Typology in the assessment and treatment of youths and families faced with the crisis of residential care, we are impelled to examine two interrelated and general hypotheses:

> *Hypothesis I:* The youth's successful completion of the residential program, as deemed by the professional staff in the program, will be explained by the family system's type, functioning, and coping as well as the youth's coping repertoire at time of entering the program. The importance of family system type, coping, and adolescent coping will remain prominent even after the powerful predictors of family and youth background are taken into consideration. The strength of these relationships will be greater than chance.

> *Hypothesis II:* The youth's successful adaptation in social settings three months after launching from the residential program, as deemed by the professional staff involved in follow-up evaluations, will be explained by the family's type, coping, and the adolescent coping repertoire. The importance of family system involvement, coping, and youth coping will remain prominent even after the powerful predictors of family and youth background are taken into consideration. The strength of this relationship will be greater than chance.

METHODOLOGY

All youths and families involved in the residential program are active participants in the program and, thus, are called upon to complete questionnaires and subjected to external observations and recordings. The information is collected throughout the period of their participation. The BOMIS system is designed to compile data at each of the phases described above. The specific research indices and measures used in the BOMIS system may be described as follows:

Background Information

Basic information includes expressions of parents' willingness to participate, youth's age, youth's race, youth's prior adjudications, and whether or not the youth has been abused physically or emotionally. This information is obtained at intake.

Family Type and Functioning

Data are obtained on the basis of standardized instruments as well as assessment of professionals. The FACES II–Family Adaptability and Cohesion Evaluation Scales (II) (Olson, Portner, & Bell, 1987) was developed to measure family cohesion and adaptability. With demonstrated internal consistency (.88 and .78, respectively) and respectable test-retest reliabilities (.80), FACES II will be used to obtain both parent and youth assessments of family functioning. Their information will be used to classify families as either balanced, mid-range, or extreme, the latter being most dysfunctional and vulnerable. Additionally, data about specific family resources of cohesion and adaptability were obtained from family members at intake and recorded in BOMIS.

Parental and Youth Coping

Central to the general hypotheses about families involved in residential care is belief in the importance of parental and family coping styles and repertoires. Parental coping was assessed through the use of F-COPES–Family Crisis Oriented Personal Evaluation Scales (McCubbin, Larsen, & Olson, 1987), a 30-item checklist of parental coping behaviors. This measure captures five coping patterns, each with respectable indices of internal consistency and test-retest reliabilities. Specifically, F-COPES measures Acquiring Social Support (.84 and .78, respectively), Reframing (.82 and .61, respectively), Seeking Spiritual Support (.81 and .95, respectively), Mobilizing Family to Acquire and Accept Help (.71 and .78, respectively), and Passive Appraisal (.86 and .81, respectively).

The youth's coping behaviors have been recorded through the use of

A-COPE–Adolescent Coping Orientation for Problem Experiences (Patterson & McCubbin, 1987). This inventory captures 12 sub-dimensions of adolescent coping, each having respectable reliabilities and validities. The subscales are: High Activity (.67), Humor (.72), Relaxation (.60), Friendship Support, Spiritual Support (.72), Professional Support (.50), Family Support and Problem Solving (.71), Ventilation (.75), Passive Problem-Solving (.71), Low Activity (.75), Emotional Connections (.76), and Self Reliance (.69).

There are multiple indicators of success in BOMIS (Whittaker, Overstreet, Grasso, Tripodi, & Boylan, 1987). In the context of this investigation, two major indices are underscored. First is the index of successful program completion. Success is defined as a professional determination of having met the expectations of the program. Unsuccessful completion would include administrative discharge or termination because a youth was unable to be handled inside the program. A court or state termination is also possible. Three-months follow-up adaptation is the second index. Three months after the youth has left the residential program, professionals conduct a follow-up assessment resulting in a calculated score which ranges from zero to twenty. This assessment is shaped by the living situation of the youths, whether or not they are in school or have graduated, whether they work, and how many police contacts they have had since termination.

In this study, data were obtained from BOMIS on a sample of 100 youths and their families, the total number of individuals and family units on which there were complete data (baseline, intake and follow-up) on all the indices depicted in Figure 1 and described under methodology. A hierarchical regression analysis was used with each discrete data set entered in the following order: Background information, family system type and functioning, family involvement in the program, family coping, and youth coping repertoires at intake. The data were also analyzed through a stepwise regression analysis with each variable entered in order of importance (unique variance explained) until the optimum list of unique predictors are identified.

RESULTS

Profile of Youth and Families

In contrast to the total sample of families and youth in BOMIS, the sub-sample of 100 families and youth appears to be representative of the

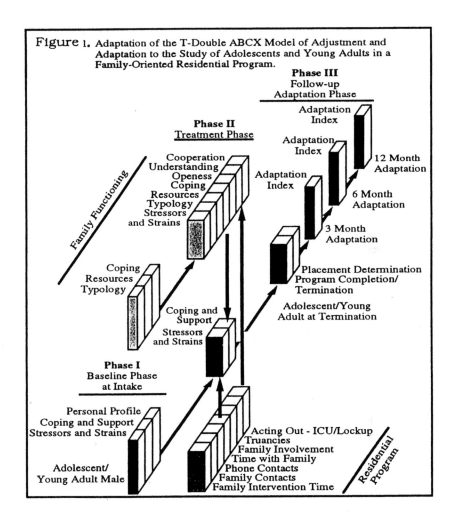

Figure 1. Adaptation of the T-Double ABCX Model of Adjustment and Adaptation to the Study of Adolescents and Young Adults in a Family-Oriented Residential Program.

total population. In general, youths are nearly equally distributed on ethnicity with slightly over half (54%) being white, over a third (39%) being black and the remainder (7%) of other ethnic groups. The average age of the youths was 15.5 years. The majority of these youths (53.2%) came from single-parent family units. Families were characterized by adult members as predominantly of the extreme type (62%), which is the most vulnerable or dysfunctional. The families were quite involved in the residential program, averaging 772 minutes of face-to-face contacts over 16 sessions, together with an average of 14 phone contacts, bringing the overall average of total family contacts to 30.

Hypothesis I is a test of the importance of family type, resources, and family involvement in explaining the youth's successful completion of the residential program. A detailed review of the hierarchical stepwise regression analysis presented in Table 1 and summarized in Figure 2 revealed the negligible importance of family and youth background factors (explaining only 3% of the variance). In general, the remaining results render partial support to the hypothesis. Family types and resources explained an additional 6% of the variance in the criterion of program completion. The expected importance of family involvement in the program was not confirmed, however, with only an additional 2% of the variance explained. Family coping (7%) and the youth's coping (15%) repertoire emerged as being the more powerful explanatory variables in understanding which youths are more likely to complete the residential program.

Carrying this analysis further to isolate critical explanatory variables, the following profile emerges: program completion appears to be explained by being a white youth coming from families with less cohesiveness or bonding, less sense of openness, less emphasis on family coping through reframing (positive outlook) as a coping strategy but, surprisingly, with a stronger family emphasis on passivity as a coping strategy. Program completion is also associated with youths' de-emphasis on coping through relaxation, friend support, and ventilation, but a stronger emphasis upon seeking professional support and spiritual support.

A more detailed analysis of a stepwise regression analysis of the same set of predictors summarized in Table 2 reveals the relative importance of a smaller set of predictors. More specifically, the criterion of program completion (19%) can be explained by family type and adolescent coping. Families at intake who are low on family cohesiveness appear to fare better in the treatment process. Additionally, adolescents who, at intake, emphasize seeking professional support but de-emphasize ventilation and friend support in their coping repertoire also appear to fare better and to complete the residential program.

Hypothesis II is a test of the importance of the same set of typology predictors in explaining the adjustment of these same youth three months after completing the program. A systematic review of the results presented in Table 3 and Figure 3 indicates that this hypothesis was supported. Background factors do not appear to be critical in the youths' post-discharge adaptation; they explain only 4% of the variance. It is useful to note, however, that black youths with a greater number of status offenses at intake have less chance of successful adaptation. Family type and resources emerged as explaining an additional 9% of the variance in a three-month adaptation. Of these variables, family cohesiveness emerges as the more important, but negatively associated explanatory variable. Family involvement in the program, expected to be critical, only explained an additional 3% of the variance.

When the family coping repertoire and the youth's coping repertoire are taken into account, the findings take on added importance. Family coping, (14%) is characterized by a strong emphasis on passive appraisal and a de-emphasis on reframing. Youth's coping (17%) is characterized by an emphasis on professional support, spiritual support, and low activity, and a de-emphasis on relaxation, family problem-solving, and ventilation.

A more detailed examination of the results of the stepwise regression analysis of the same variables reaffirms the relative importance of family cohesiveness along with family and adolescent coping. The analysis also isolates the critical predictions with the resulting profile. Youth adaptation three months following program completion is explained by being part of a family unit that is low on cohesiveness and bonding and emphasizes passive appraisal as a dominant coping strategy. Adaptation is also related to youths' emphasis on coping by seeking professional and spiritual support. In contrast, adaptation was related to youths' de-emphasis upon ventilation and relaxation as a major part of their coping repertoire at intake.

DISCUSSION

Since the treatment strategy of the Boysville program is committed to structural family therapy at this stage in the program's development and the database is weighted heavily to include this exceptional body of family information, the findings of this investigation take on added importance. One could interpret these to indicate relatively strong support for an emphasis on family system functioning as an appropriate target for intervention even in the context of residential treatment for deviant youth.

In exploring sources of successful program completion, family type and resources emerged with considerable visibility in explaining 6% of the variance. However, the critical element in family type appears to be the degree to which the family unit is bonded together, its cohesiveness. The more the family appraises itself as being closely knit as a unit, the less the probability that the youth will complete the program. These findings point to the underlying family dynamics of enmeshment operating within these family units, with the youth seemingly trapped in, but struggling to disengage himself from, the stifling web of family togetherness. The Circum-

TABLE 1. Hierarchical regression analysis of family typology variables in explaining adolescent/youth coping before completion of residential program

N= 100

Predictors	R	R²	F	p=	Beta	r
Background						
Parent's Willingness to Participate					-.08	-.08
Youth's Felonies at Intake					.00	.00
Youth's Age					-.02	-.01
Abused before Intake					-.03	-.02
Number of Status Offenses					.00	.02
Ethnicity: Black	.17	.03	.49	.81	-.16*	-.16
Family Type & Resources						
Balanced Family Type					-.07	-.05
Family Adaptability					-.08	-.13
Extreme Family Type					.10	.13
Family Cohesiveness	.31	.09	.92	.52	-.30*	-.25
Family Involvement in Program						
Intensity					.05	.02
Understanding					-.04	.02
Cooperation					-.11	.01
Openess	.33	.11	.74	.73	-.21*	-.05

Family Coping Patterns at Intake

Coping: Social Support				-.03	-.08
Coping: Spiritual Support				.01	.07
Coping: Reframing				-.12*	-.19
Coping: Passive Appraisal				.29*	.10
Coping: Mobilizing For Help	.42	.18	.90	.58	-.09	-.15

Youth Coping at Intake

Coping: Humor				-.06	-.07
Coping: High Activity				-.00	.02
Coping: Relaxation				-.20*	-.16
Coping: Professional Support				.21*	.18
Coping: Friend Support				-.13*	-.14
Coping: Spiritual Support				.20*	.06
Coping: Family Problem Solving				.05	.00
Coping: Ventilation				-.27*	-.14
Coping: Passive Appraisal				.19*	.06
Coping: Emotional Connections				.08	.06
Coping: Low Activity				.10	.03
Coping: Self Reliance	.57	.33	1.06	.41	-.09	.01

*p ≤ .01

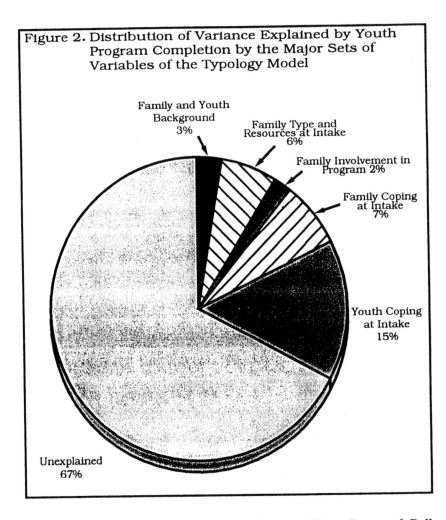

Figure 2. Distribution of Variance Explained by Youth Program Completion by the Major Sets of Variables of the Typology Model

Family and Youth Background 3%

Family Type and Resources at Intake 6%

Family Involvement in Program 2%

Family Coping at Intake 7%

Youth Coping at Intake 15%

Unexplained 67%

plex Model used to guide the study of family types (Olson, Portner, & Bell 1987) gains additional value in the context of this study and program. This finding and inference mode also renders additional support for, and clarity to, the residential program's emphasis on structural family therapy, which is designed to focus on these specific underlying processes that have been shown to be troubling to children, youths, and parents.

The surprising emergence of parental and youth coping presents new challenges to both theory-building and service provision to these families

TABLE 2. Stepwise regression analysis of family typology variables with the criterion of adolescent program completion

Predictors	R	R^2	F	p=	Beta	r
Family Type						
Family Cohesion	.25	.06	6.45	.01	-.25	-.25
Adolescent Coping						
Ventilation	.33	.11	5.84	.004	-.22	-.14
Professional Support	.37	.14	5.22	.012	.18	.18
Friend support	.43	.19	5.53	.0001	-.23	-.14

TABLE 3. Hierarchial regression analysis of typology variables to explain three-months following program completion

N= 100

Predictors	R	R²	F	p=	Beta	r
Background						
Parent's Willingness to Participate					-.11	-.11
Youth's Felonies at Intake					.02	.03
Youth's Age					-.04	-.03
Abused before Intake					.01	.02
Number of Status Offenses					-.12*	-.08
Ethnicity: Black	.21	.04	.74	.62	-.14*	-.13
Family Type & Resources						
Balanced Family Type					.02	.05
Family Adaptability					-.06	-.10
Extreme Family Type					.07	.04
Family Cohesiveness	.36	.13	1.36	.21	-.40*	-.26
Family Involvement in Program						
Intensity					.06	.04
Understanding					.03	.07
Cooperation					.01	.07
Openess	.40	.16	1.14	.33	-.33*	-.02

Family Coping Patterns at Intake

Coping: Social Support				.05	-.02
Coping: Spiritual Support				.09	.01
Coping: Reframing				-.13*	-.17
Coping: Passive Appraisal				.42*	.26
Coping: Mobilizing For Help	.55	.30	1.81	.04 / -.11	-.13

Youth Coping at Intake

Coping: Humor				.06	.01
Coping: High Activity				.03	.09
Coping: Relaxation				-.20*	-.15
Coping: Professional Support				.19*	.21
Coping: Friend Support				-.04	-.04
Coping: Spiritual Support				.31*	.17
Coping: Family Problem Solving				-.16*	-.05
Coping: Ventilation				-.29*	-.16
Coping: Passive Appraisal				-.01	-.02
Coping: Emotional Connections				.07	.10
Coping: Low Activity				.15*	.11
Coping: Self Reliance	.69	.47	1.97	.01 / .04	.09

*p ≤ .01

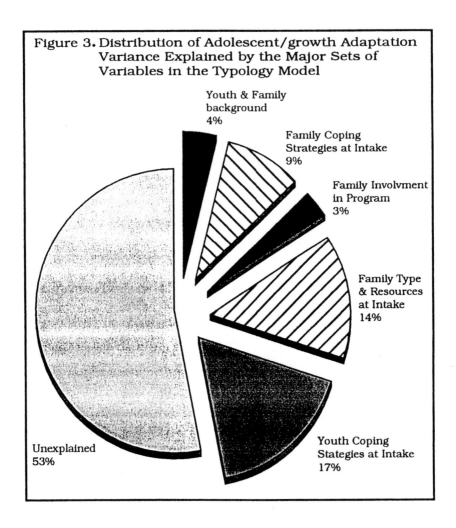

Figure 3. Distribution of Adolescent/growth Adaptation Variance Explained by the Major Sets of Variables in the Typology Model

and youths. From the perspective of the Typology Model of Family Adjustment and Adaptation (McCubbin & McCubbin, 1988), we can affirm that the hypotheses derived from the model are viable and relevant. We can also affirm the realization that there is a complex interplay between family type, family functioning, family involvement, parental coping, and youth coping. But the discovery of the enduring importance of parental and youth coping both in relationship to program completion and three-month adaptation encourages us to explore further to understand the nature of coping in the context of a residential program. We are pressed to explore and understand the interaction between parental and youth coping. We are challenged to examine how the Boysville program can strengthen its emphasis on expanding the coping capacities of its youth.

Adolescents or young adults who emphasize seeking professional support, spiritual support, and low activity as major themes in their repertoire at intake appear to fare better both during and following treatment. These findings emphasize the importance of "fit" between the youth entering treatment and what the residential program emphasizes and offers. In this case, the strengths of the youths' coping repertoire appears to complement Boysville's focus on professional support and modeling, spiritual support, and planful use of activities as integral parts of residential care and treatment.

In contrast, the youth's emphasis on coping through ventilation (i.e., swearing, open expression of anger), friend support, relaxation, and family-problem-solving at intake appears to predispose the youth against both successful program completion and post-treatment adaptation. When we consider how difficult it is to identify valid predictors of post-treatment adaptation, these observations take on greater importance. It would appear that youths who depend upon profanity and verbal hostility and rely on friends who are also likely to be struggling and to continue to struggle with their families, apparently with little satisfaction, have continued difficulty within the Boysville program and post-discharge.

By design, BOMIS involved the systematic sharing of information from the management system with staff; youth coping profiles were among the information shared. Is it reasonable to assume that professional staff in the residential program, once exposed to the data, planfully or unconsciously developed an approach to cultivate coping in their youthful clients? In parents? Understandably, one may hypothesize that service to youths and families may have been altered and shaped by the sharing of coping data, and thus the influence of parental and youth coping on adaptation can be understood.

On the other hand, we need to consider whether we do enough to support parents and youths to facilitate their coping. Is it possible that we have a rather limited technology to support parents and youth on coping, and that the results we observed suggest that the family's and youth's coping repertoire really made the difference without the benefits of the focused residential program? In any case, the importance of parental and youth coping cannot be ignored or treated lightly in the future. Clearly, youth coping should become a stronger focus of the residential program.

But parental coping as an adjunct to structural family therapy can also benefit from additional thought and planning.

BOMIS has already provided an empirical base for clinical and program evaluation as well as practice innovations. It could also lead to a restructuring of our approach to both parents and youth, with a greater emphasis upon improving their problem-solving and coping skills and sense of personal confidence and well-being.

This emphasis upon parental and youth coping encourages us to reexamine the treatment paradigm. In contrast to past research and treatment paradigms, with their emphasis on what makes families break down or deteriorate in response to the change and stress, the findings of this investigation place a much greater emphasis on family strengths, capabilities, and coping. These emerge as distinct targets for future intervention. Instead of resolving family conflicts, the new paradigm would be closer to that of family life educators who see what is good about families even at their weakest moment (see Olson, McCubbin, Barnes, Larsen, Muxem, & Wilson, 1983). If we adopt a family strengths, parental coping, and youth coping orientation with an increased emphasis upon what makes parents and youths successful, we can anticipate a significant shift in theory and research, not to mention clinical intervention.

REFERENCES

Conrad, K. (1985). Promoting quality of care: The role of the compliance director. *Child Welfare, 64,* 639-649.

Epstein, I., & Grasso, A. (1987). Integrating management information and program evaluation: The Boysville experience. In J. Morton, M. L. Ballasone, & S. Guendelman (Eds.), *Preventing low birthweight and infant mortality: Programmatic issues for public health social workers*, Berkeley: University of California.

Fanshel, D. (1977). Parental visiting of foster children: A computerized study. *Social Work Research Abstracts, 13,* 2-10.

McCubbin, H., Larsen, A., & Olson, D. (1987). F-COPES: Family crisis oriented personal evaluation scales. In H. McCubbin & A. Thompson (Eds.), *Family assessment inventories for research and practice* (pp. 195-210). Madison: University of Wisconsin.

McCubbin, H., & McCubbin, M. (1988). Typologies of resilient families: Emerging rules and social class and ethnicity. *Family Relations, 37,* 247-254.

McCubbin, M., & McCubbin, H. (1987). Family stress theory and assessment: The T-Double ABCX model of family adjustment and adaptation. In H. McCubbin & A. Thompson (Eds.), *Family assessment inventories for research and practice.* Madison: University of Wisconsin, pp. 2-32.

Olson, D., McCubbin, H., Barnes, H., Larsen, A., Muxem, A., & Wilson, M.

(1983). *Families: What makes them work?* Beverly Hills, CA: Sage Publications.

Olson, D., Portner, J., & Bell, R. (1987). FACES II: Family adaptability and cohesion evaluation scales. In H. McCubbin & A. Thompson (Eds.), *Family assessment inventories for research and practice* (pp. 63-78). Madison: University of Wisconsin.

Patterson, J., & McCubbin, H. (1987). Adolescent coping styles and behaviors, conceptualization, and measurement. *Journal of Adolescence, 10,* 163-186.

Whittaker, J. K., Overstreet, E., Grasso, A., Tripodi, T., & Boylan, F. (1987). Multiple indicators of success in residential youth care and treatment. *American Journal of Orthopsychiatry, 58,* 143-147.

Index